Thy Kingdom Come

Lent and Easter Sermons

by

David H. Petersen

Copyright © 2012 Emmanuel Press
Fort Wayne, Indiana
www.emmanuelpress.us
emmanuelpress@gmail.com

Cover Art:
Crucifixion fresco from the Imperial Cathedral of Speyer, Germany
Photograph Copyright © 2007 Michael N. Frese

Author Photograph:
Photograph Copyright © 2012 Steve Blakey, B&B Design
bbdesign@mindspring.com

ISBN 978-1-934328-07-1

For the saints who came in the dark of night,
through rain, snow, and worse, early in the morning,
to hear God's Word and receive His holy Sacrament,
and who, along the way, endured these sermons
as though they were equal to the task and space.

໙

Table of Contents

Forward

Stealing is a sin. And since no one reads a forward except its author and editor, I can safely admit it here: I am guilty of stealing. I have stolen more textual insights and sermon ideas from Pastor David Petersen than I can remember. Why? I want to be a really good preacher.

Eventually, though, you have to stop looking for individual ideas and phrases to steal and start wondering, "What is this preacher doing that makes his preaching so good?" In Pr. Petersen's case, I haven't completely cracked the code, but I do have a short list.

This preacher knows his text. I have heard him do more with the Greek conjunction *kai* than most other preachers do with an entire column of text. Pr. Petersen knows the text isn't a springboard, but the pool. He immerses himself and his hearers in the stuff of the text, the words.

This preacher knows his people. He preaches for his people, not for professors, other pastors, or posterity. As a young preacher, many of my sermons were delivered to my parishioners, but they were written for my former seminary professors and fellow pastors—none of whom were there to hear. Pr. Petersen's audience is in the pews.

This preacher knows himself. His preaching is brutally honest. When Pr. Petersen preaches the Law against sin, I'm quite sure he's speaking from personal reflection. When he preaches the Gospel, he is just as happy to hear it as the rest of us.

This preacher knows the Word does all the work. I never get the impression that Pr. Petersen is trying to turn out a masterpiece. His sermons are rough-cut from the text. Despite his considerable skill, he knows that his skill adds absolutely nothing to his preaching.

We often evaluate the quality of sermons based on all the wrong things: I wasn't offended, I agree with what the pastor said, it kept me interested, or any number of shallow observations. There is nothing wrong with being interested in a sermon, but that is not the touchstone. A lot of things are interesting, but that doesn't necessarily make them good.

This is the hallmark of a good sermon: Does it preach Jesus Christ crucified for you, a sinner? If it doesn't, no matter how good it may be in other respects, it is not a good sermon. St. Paul himself said, "For I decided to know nothing among you except Jesus Christ and him crucified" (1 Cor. 2:2). Jesus requires this of his preachers. He charges His Church with the task of preaching repentance and the forgiveness of sins in His Name to all nations (Luke 24:47).

In a good sermon, we should actually lose track of how often Jesus is mentioned. And when He is mentioned, He should be the subject of the verbs, the one doing the actions. And then pay attention: What are those verbs? Do they make Jesus sound like a coach, a therapist, an advisor—or your Savior? Listen for the verbs that Scripture gives to Jesus—the Jesus who lives for you, suffers for you, dies for you, bleeds for you, gives His life for you, is your substitute, and rises again for you. These are the verbs you ought to be hearing if in fact your pastor preaches Christ crucified.

As it should be, every one of Pr. Petersen's sermons is a bloody mess of Law and Gospel. The mess of your sin and the mess of Jesus' cross are on display in every sermon. No matter the occasion, no matter the readings, every sermon is about Jesus in His saving work, Jesus crucified for you. All of Scripture testifies to Jesus; it all points to Him. So too should sermons.

I believe that we are both burdened and blessed to live in a time of the worst and best preaching the Church as ever known. Pr. Petersen's is among the best.

I want to be a really good preacher. So I will go on stealing from Pr. Petersen, and I hope if you are a preacher and haven't already, you will begin to do so too. This book is your opportunity.

But whether you are a hearer or a preacher, I pray this book does for you what it has done for me. For there is far more here than mere textual insights and sermon ideas; here is the Gospel for sinners. This book delivers Christ crucified for sinners. And we all need that.

Rev. Todd Wilken, host
Issues, Etc. Radio Show

Introduction

Thy kingdom come. What does this mean? As Luther explains in the Small Catechism, we are asking for our heavenly Father to give us the Holy Spirit so that we believe His holy Word. The Holy Spirit is given to us through preaching and the Holy Sacraments, which begin and cultivate our faith. When God gave the Holy Spirit to the apostles on Pentecost, the first thing they did was preach. Each person heard the apostles preaching in his own language, thereby undoing the curse of Babel. The apostles went forth from Pentecost, preaching and giving the Holy Spirit so that God's kingdom would come to the people.

> The coming of God's kingdom to us occurs in two ways; first, here in time through the Word and faith; and secondly, in eternity forever through revelation. Now we pray for both these things, that it may come to those who are not yet in it, and, by daily increase, to us who have received the same, and hereafter in eternal life. All this is nothing else than saying: Dear Father, we pray, give us first Thy Word, that the Gospel be preached properly throughout the world; and secondly, that it be received in faith, and work and live in us, so that through the Word and the power of the Holy Ghost Thy kingdom may prevail among us, and the kingdom of the devil be put down, that he may have no right or power over us, until at last it shall be utterly destroyed, and sin, death, and hell shall be exterminated, that we may live forever in perfect righteousness and blessedness. (Martin Luther, Large Catechism – Second Petition, *Triglotta*, 1917)

Luther emphasizes that the kingdom of God comes through the preaching of His Word. By this preaching, the Holy Spirit causes the kingdom of heaven to prevail over against the kingdom of the devil, converting those who do not yet believe and strengthening those who have already come to faith. It is missional and edifying—evangelical in the strictest use of the word. The Law brings us to a recognition of our sin, the world, and the devil; by God's grace, repentance then follows. The Gospel subsequently forgives, soothes, and comforts terrified consciences. Preaching brings the kingdom of heaven from Christ, through the Holy Spirit, to the individual. For preaching is pure application of God's Word.

Thus, when we pray in the second petition for God's kingdom to come, we are not primarily praying for a release or removal from this world but rather for God to enter into our world, and indeed our lives, by preaching and His Word. This He does through the sending of the Holy Spirit, who brings to remembrance all that Christ has done as we confess in the Second Article of the Apostles' Creed: Jesus was conceived by the Holy Spirit, born of the Virgin Mary, suffered under Pontius Pilate, was crucified, died, and was buried. On the third day He rose again, ascended into heaven, and sits at the right hand of God until He comes again to judge the living and the dead. This is the focus and message which the Holy Spirit delivers through the mouths of preachers. Since the kingdom of heaven is nothing else than every deed and act of Jesus in His incarnation, true Gospel preaching, then, is nothing else than a delivery of the heavenly kingdom. St. Paul writes that the kingdom of God is "righteousness and peace and joy in the Holy Spirit" (Rom. 14:17).

Yet in this petition, we are in a secondary sense praying for a godly end to our lives in this world. By praying for God's kingdom to come, we are praying for the Holy Spirit to prepare us for Christ's return in judgment. The proper preparation for this is by hearing God's Word in preaching, which gives faith and increases faith in those hearing. And it is only by faith that we are prepared for eternal life.

Thy Kingdom Come is a title rich in the birth, crucifixion, and resurrection of Christ. It is rich in the sending of the Holy Spirit and the preaching of God's Word, in the initiation and strengthening of faith, in the joyful expectation for us to join the multitudes around Christ's throne. The petition "Thy kingdom come" expresses the desire of the Christian for the Father to send the Holy Spirit to breathe the life and love of Christ into our nostrils, speak Christ into our ears, and keep Christ dwelling in us until the Lord comes again.

ABOUT THE BOOK

The process of compiling these Lent and Easter sermons is several years in the making. Knowing the regular rhythm of worship at Redeemer Lutheran Church in Fort Wayne, I asked Pr. Petersen about publishing a book of sermons for the forty days of Lent. It is the custom at Redeemer to have services every day, including four weekly Divine Services and Matins six days a week. During daily Matins, there is a reading from the Fathers. However, during penitential seasons, daily Matins is laid aside in favor of the daily Eucharist, and original sermons are preached in place of the readings from the Fathers.

This book arises from the culture of an active parish life as a part of its usual worship routine. These sermons were developed during the Lenten seasons of 2011 and 2012 but were edited and polished in the summer of 2012. Pr. Petersen began preaching and recording his sermons during 2011, but with the rigors of preaching daily along with regular parish duties, he was not able to write down every sermon he delivered that year. During 2012, he revised and expanded the texts he had written the previous year and wrote down the remaining sermons. Since he has been preaching daily during the penitential seasons for over 10 years, this homiletical material has been percolating and developing over years of preaching on these texts.

Along with the daily sermons in Lent, I have also included the Pre-Lent Sunday sermons, meaning the three Sundays prior to Ash Wednesday according to the historic one-year lectionary which Redeemer follows. Then follow the sermons from the Sundays after Easter up to Pentecost as well as several from saints' days whose specific dates fall in or near the seasons of Lent or Easter.

One of the distinct marks of Pr. Petersen's preaching style is the ease with which he moves between his own words and the words of Holy Scripture. He interweaves the language of the sacred text fluidly throughout each sermon. It would, therefore, be a daunting task and cumbersome in appearance to cite every Biblical reference, not to mention out of sync with the rhythm and smoothness of his preaching. When Pr. Petersen preaches, he does not typically cite passages chapter and verse; a Scriptural reference or allusion is left for the listener to glean. He preaches to a broad range of Christians in one context. The newest Christian to the most theologically astute can understand the Law and the Gospel applied specifically to him. It is one reason that his own parishioners, including families and individuals as well as seminary faculty, students, and visitors, find his preaching so edifying.

The daily lectionary for Lent is found in *Daily Divine Service Book: A Lutheran Daily Missal*, edited by Pr. Heath R. Curtis. Each sermon is primarily based upon the Gospel readings, but the content is, of course, influenced by the other readings. Whenever Pr. Petersen quotes directly from Holy Scripture and the quote is not part of one of the assigned readings for that day, I have added a Scriptural citation. All direct quotes are from the ESV, unless otherwise noted. Because *Daily Divine Service Book* uses the KJV for its weekday propers, this translation has naturally shaped his words, quotes, and allusions.

I also labored over capitalization, attempting to maintain consistency and reverence. Because reading a sermon is different from listening to a sermon, I felt that capitalizing every reference or allusion to God the Father, Son, and Holy Spirit would be distracting to the reader. I primarily looked to the ESV as a guide to capitalization, with the modification of capitalizing divine pronouns and the occasional Messianic metaphor, when necessary for clarification.

I suggest that you read the assigned readings for the day to put the sermon in its proper Biblical context. For God's kingdom comes when He sends His Holy Spirit, who works through the written and preached Word to show Christ and Him crucified, died, and risen.

> But we preach Christ crucified, unto the Jews a stumbling block, and unto the Greeks foolishness; but unto them which are called, both Jews and Greeks, Christ the power of God, and the wisdom of God. (1 Cor. 1:23-24 KJV)

Rev. Michael N. Frese
Emmanuel Press
Redeemer Lutheran Church
Fort Wayne, Indiana

Septuagesima

Exodus 17:1-7
1 Corinthians 9:24-10:5
St. Matthew 20:1-16

In the name of the Father and of the ✠ Son and of the Holy Spirit. Amen.

The main point of the parable is that entrance into the kingdom comes by grace. The workers are rewarded for work they did not perform. This is hardly a surprise to us; in fact, we practically expect it.

G.K. Chesterton once said, "Do not be proud of the fact that your grandmother was shocked at something which you are accustomed to seeing or hearing without being shocked…It may be that your grandmother was an extremely lively and vital animal and that you are a paralytic."

Chesterton has in mind immoral things. He means, "Don't think you are more sophisticated than your grandmother because you watch television shows full of vulgarities and aren't bothered by them. It could be that she was highly intelligent and sensitive and you have been paralyzed by evil so much that you don't even notice it."

The same sort of numbness applies to the Gospel as well. I fear that it is even worse. We're not just numb, but we've crossed over the line drawn by Bonhoeffer into "cheap grace." I fear we're now guilty of thinking grace is worse than cheap: It is a right, an entitlement, as though God owed us salvation. Repent.

That is what was wrong with the workers who worked all day and grumbled. They thought they were entitled to more. They weren't asking for grace, but for justice. They thought that they deserved to be rewarded. Thus their eyes were evil. Their eyes were evil because the owner was good.

We come along and think we are entitled to grace; that is simply what is just. Everyone should go to heaven. Sins shouldn't matter. Everyone deserves a chance. "Don't judge" is our greatest cause and virtue.

Repent. This parable is a warning.

God isn't like you. He doesn't think the way you think. His ways are not your ways. And He doesn't owe you, or anyone, anything. For reasons all His own, however, He loves and welcomes you into His kingdom—not for free, but for the bloody, torturous death of His beloved Son. This is the essence of the Gospel: The Lord rewards those who don't deserve it. He loves those who hate and abuse Him. He gives gifts to those who steal from Him. He is generous, merciful, and good despite you. If that doesn't send a tingle down your spine, and you haven't just lost a baby or your mother, shame on you. The Gospel doesn't promise an emotional reaction, but it almost always gives it. The Bible calls that emotion joy.

At the time of our Lord there was another parable in vogue, one that sounded a lot like His. It had been told at the funeral of a prominent rabbi who died at just twenty-eight years old. A certain king had servants working in a field for the day. After two hours he took one of the servants by the hand and walked up and down the rows with him, offering him refreshments and such while the others worked. At the end of the day, the king had his foreman line up and pay all the workers, including this man who only worked two hours out of twelve. Like our Lord's parable, all of the workers were paid the same amount. Then some of those who had worked all day complained; they thought they should get more than the man who only worked two hours. The king responded that the servant he favored had done as much in two hours as the others did in a full day. So it was fair. The point was that the young rabbi who had died was being rewarded early because he was so good.†

The moral here is that God will reward us according to our work, and if you can cram seventy years of good works into twenty-eight, then you can go to heaven early. I wouldn't want to deny that rabbi's family comfort. There is a truth in what that parable teaches. There is justice in rewards for works. But that is the expected thing. The rabbi's parable is about fair wages, paying according to work done, not according to time or grace.

Our Lord's parable takes a markedly different turn, doesn't it? He isn't teaching fair wages or justice. He is teaching grace. In our Lord's parable the workers who stood in the marketplace idle all day got paid as though they worked all day. The young rabbi was rewarded for doing excellent work and working quickly. These bums were rewarded the same as he was. He didn't get grace; rather, he got what he deserved. He worked fast, so he was paid early. But that is not what the kingdom of God is like. The kingdom of God is where bums who don't work get rewards for the work of others.

God's way is no way to run a business. Businesses cannot afford to pay workers who don't work. But this is the way God runs the universe. Even the unbelievers benefit from His grace. The worst existence on earth is better than what we all deserve in hell. Even unbelievers enjoy good things in creation, like sunshine and water and food. The Lord owes us nothing. Every good thing—coffee and biscuits and swing sets and puppies and a dry towel—is a gift and comes from God's mercy.

Those who worked all day got what was just, what they had bargained for. In the end, however, that is a terrible thing. For even if they did bear the heat and brunt of the day, they are sent away with only what is theirs. Perhaps they enjoyed some glimpses of good in

---

† This parable is related by Alfred Edersheim in *The Life and Times of Jesus the Messiah* Vol. 2. (Grand Rapids: Wm. B. Eerdmans, 1947), p. 420.

the vineyard while they worked, but then they are sent away with only what they earned.

How sad and terrible! What is ours, what we've fully earned, is damnation for our sins. Kyrie Eleison!

The other workers came on the basis of a promise. The owner simply said, "Come to the vineyard, and what is right I will give you." He did not tell them how much. No doubt, they expected less than a full day's wages. But they came on faith, trusting that the owner would be good to them. And there is more: Not only are they paid at the end more than they deserved, but they also remain with the owner. They are not sent away. They came by faith, are paid what they do not deserve, and then remain by the owner's on-going goodness and mercy. That remaining is no small detail.

This is the defining character of the kingdom. Grace is undeserved and unearned, even unexpected. For even when we are caught in our selfish thoughts of entitlement, we do not have the ability to expect the full goodness and generosity of the Lord. Grace exceeds even the desires of our selfish hearts. Our cups overflow. He gives us His Son, His risen body and blood. The workers didn't expect a full day's wage. They got that unexpected, undeserved wage and more. They got a place at His table, His daughter's hand, an inheritance and honor.

We are no longer mere workers being overpaid. By grace, we are now members of the family, co-owners of the kingdom, the bride of the Son. We remain with Him. May God in His mercy keep this ever new to and for us, that our hearts would not grow cold or take His grace for granted. May He keep us ever mindful of the cost of His love in the death of the Son and the fulfillment of His love in the resurrection as He provides once again in His risen body and blood.

In ✠ Jesus' name. Amen.

SEXAGESIMA

Isaiah 55:10-13
2 Corinthians 11:19-12:9
St. Luke 8:4-15

In the name of the Father and of the ✠ Son and of the Holy Spirit. Amen.

The path, the rock, and then the thorns—that is the deliberate order of the parable. First the path because the first thing we need is recollection and caution. We need to pay attention and listen closely to the Word of God and not forget it, lest it be snatched away from us. If our faith is based upon anything other than the Word of God, it is in vain. So we must be careful, reverent, and deliberate hearers.

Next comes the rock. We need fortitude. If the faith planted in us is not tended by the Word and Sacraments, it will wither and die. Faith has no strength in itself. Even as we cannot forget God's Word, neither can we neglect it. It is not enough to have once believed.

Finally come the thorns. We need contempt for things present. Even St. Paul was prone to this world's allure. That is why he wrote, as we read last week, that he disciplined his body lest after he preached to others, he himself would fall away. Our bodies, our physical lives, as well as our desire for honor, prestige, and love among men are a threat to our faith.

This last threat, worry, is the worst and most applicable to us who have been brought together today by the Holy Spirit to hear His Word and receive the risen body and blood of Christ. Though we are not without fault, still we are not careless or forgetful hearers. We have been baptized. So also, though we are not perfect, we are not completely negligent of what God has given. We are here—no matter how long we've been absent—for what God gives and to hear His Word.

Yet even so, even though we are baptized, careful hearers of God's Word, we feel the strong pull of the flesh: worries, riches, and pleasures. We have all succumbed, even in the course of this service. Our minds have wandered. Our bodies have pulled. Our daydreams are not pure. Neither are our plans. Repent.

Worries, riches, and pleasures are signified in the parable by thorns. Worries, riches, and pleasures prick and lacerate the mind. Sin is like methamphetamine or crack. It gives a temporary, unworldly, and costly burst of bliss, but in doing so it enslaves the perpetrator. Now his thoughts and heart are deformed. He no longer finds any joy in joyful things. He only longs for the unworldly bliss of the drug. It never satisfies him, and it takes everything else away. Sin fills the sinner with anxiety over when he will next taste of it and how he might keep and gain more of it for himself. Sin stops joyful things from being joyful. Thorns do not prick and then let go; they entangle and trap. Sin is a barbed thorn.

He who has ears to hear, let him hear. This parable is not about why some believe and others don't. It is a parable of warning for those who know the mysteries of the kingdom of God.

It is also an illustration of God's grace in Christ. The good ground bears fruit through patience. Nothing we do is good unless we endure it patiently. The Christ Himself suffered all things the parable describes. He was driven by the Holy Spirit to the desolate place, to places well trod by demons. There He shows Himself a ready hearer when He says to Satan, "Man shall not live by bread alone, but by every word that comes from the mouth of God" (Matt. 4:4). There, and again upon the cross, He was parched and thirsty and went without finding sustenance in the promise of God. Then at His trial, and on the cross, He bore the thorns for us. He is our king who has taken our place, who has endured our punishment to spare us His own wrath. He has been tempted in all the ways that we are tempted and has borne it all with perfect patience, without sin. We are the hundredfold fruit that He produces, a gift to His Father.

This is why the Lord sows His seed so recklessly. The fruit that He seeks is already bought and paid for. He sows where no reasonable sower would sow: on the trodden path, in rocky and thorny ground. And His Word does what no ordinary sower could expect of his seed. It transforms the ground. It bears fruit in the unlikely hearts of rebellious men. He sows because He is good and His seed is good and we need it.

He is no respecter of persons and does not discriminate. He sows His seed lavishly, inviting all those with ears to hear. No one comes to this kingdom worthily. There are no good people, no plowed and ready ground. There are only sinners. Some are stubborn and deny that they are sinners or deny that Jesus is the Lord's Christ. But some—by grace, not because they are good or smart, but because He is good—are transformed and acknowledge their need for grace and the lordship of Jesus Christ. He who has gets more. The kingdom is not built on justice, but on grace.

The first part of the parable shows us what we need. We need to pay attention and listen closely to the Word of God. We need the Word and Sacraments to nourish the faith that He has given. And we need a certain contempt for and detachment from things present. Without these things, we will be snatched by demons, dried and withered, and choked out.

The last bit of the parable bestows all these things in the liberality of the sower. We are not simply commanded to stop worrying, but all real cause for worry is removed. God satisfied His own Law on our behalf. He is not stingy with His saving Word of grace. He provides all that we need and more. He forgives our sins. He strengthens our faith. He enlightens our hearts and minds by grace. He drives off the demon birds that seek to snatch and peck at us.

The holy Word, the Seed of God, the Christ born of Mary, crucified and risen from the dead, is here for us in bread and wine, calling us once again. He who has ears to hear, let him hear.

In ✠ Jesus' name. Amen.

QUINQUAGESIMA

1 Samuel 16:1-13
1 Corinthians 13:1-13
St. Luke 18:31-43

In the name of the Father and of the ✠ *Son and of the Holy Spirit. Amen.*

Our Lord's third and final prediction of His coming crucifixion in Jerusalem could hardly be more explicit or clear. Everything that is written about the Son of Man by the prophets will be accomplished. Between our Lord's own clear predictions, the entire history of Israel, and all that the prophets wrote, there should be no real surprises. But it is not hard to surprise a blind man, and the disciples are blind.

That doesn't stop the Lord. Thanks be to God! He doesn't need their understanding. They are not worthy of His love, but that doesn't stop Him either. He loves them anyway.

As they make their way through Jericho, a crowd gathers. A blind man, named Bartimaeus by St. Mark, asks who is coming and is told only, "Jesus of Nazareth." But the blind man reveals his sight. He will not be hushed. He cries not for alms, but for mercy. He cries not to some rabbi or miracle worker, but to the Son of David, the One who goes to Jerusalem as a sacrifice, the One who rules as king by grace and mercy.

He who hears the cries of all who are distressed hears the blind man. He commands that he be brought to Him. Then He asks him, "What do you want Me to do for you?" The blind man gives the obvious answer: "To recover my sight." The Lord says, "Recover your sight. Your faith has saved you." The now seeing man follows along to Jerusalem, glorifying God.

Here is what we are usually blind to: If the blind man gains his sight, he loses his employment and way of life. It is easy for us, of course, to realize that life with sight is better than blindness, but we're on the other side of it. The blind man has a pretty good thing going. Is he willing to risk it?

Socrates' most famous allegory is that of the cave. A group of people have lived chained to the wall of a cave all of their lives, facing a blank wall. These people watch shadows projected on the wall by things passing in front of a fire behind them. They never see real things. They only see the shadows, thus they think the shadows are reality. Socrates explains that the philosopher is like a prisoner who has been freed from the cave and has learned that the shadows on the wall are not reality. But when he goes back to tell the other prisoners, they don't believe him and even kill him. The point is this: People don't like having their worldview challenged.

Socrates is on to something. Blindness can be comfortable. When the Lord asks the blind man what he wants Him to do for him, it is not that the Lord is uncertain. Why, then, does He ask? He wants to be sure that the blind man knows what he is in for. It is not at all unlike the baptism rite when we ask the child, "Will you be baptized?"

Why do we ask that? Because Holy Baptism is going to take you out of the cave, and you can never go back. This will make the devil a lifelong enemy. You will no longer sit by the side of the road with your friends. You will go to bloody, traitorous Jerusalem. The servant is not above the master. "Pick up your cross and follow Me" means "Come, die with Me."

To be sure, the blind man sees more clearly than the disciples. He recognizes the way to life through death. They follow with their feet, but their hearts are not in it. They are still too attached to this world. Who isn't? They wanted a miracle worker—not a sacrifice. They wanted a teacher who would blow their minds with insightful teaching—not a Messiah. The blind man recognizes Jesus of Nazareth as the long-foretold Son of David. He sees where they are blind. He knows the cost, but he also sees the value. So he gives up his life, everything that he had known, and he follows Jesus to the gallows in Jerusalem, glorifying God.

The hateful gallows of Jerusalem are the most beautiful architecture ever erected on earth. They are the tree of life, from whence comes our life with God. During the Stations of the Cross, over and over again we say, "We adore Thee, O Christ, and we praise Thee. Because by Thy holy cross, Thou hast redeemed the world."

What has all this to do with us? We mourn for our sins. We have been selfish, greedy, impatient, angry, lustful, and full of pride. We have hurt ourselves and our loved ones. We have failed to serve and love our neighbors. Let us repent and set our faces toward Jerusalem. Ash Wednesday looms close. We prepare for the journey. For we know that we have been too attached to this world, too afraid to leave behind the pleasures of the flesh. We are desperately in need of a Savior.

But for all that, let us not sorrow for the love of God that has sent the Son to be handed over to the Gentiles, to be mocked, shamefully treated, spit upon, flogged, and crucified. In that, rather, let us give thanks and rejoice. Let us be like the cured blind man, following to Jerusalem, glorifying God, knowing that leaving behind our sins is like leaving behind blindness. What do you want? To be free of sin, O Lord.

We go to Jerusalem, for there on the holy cross is the love of God that would not bend or turn. There is the love that purifies and saves and declares sinners like us to be the saints of God. Let us not forget the end of that prophecy, now known in history, that for all the sorrows and hell that our Lord suffered, on the third day He rose again. We go to Jerusalem not just because there Jesus pays for our sins but also because Jesus lives.

Whether we understand these things as well as the blind man or are as confused and stubborn, uncertain and fearful as the disciples, let us follow to Jerusalem and the holy cross of Jesus Christ. We follow Him not simply by some effort of the imagination, but we follow Him by partaking of His holy body and blood. Here is the fruit of the cross, the gift of the resurrection.

What do you want? To recover sight? To be free of sin? Or perhaps simply to be with You, O Lord, wherever You may be and wherever You may lead.

In ✠ *Jesus' name. Amen.*

Ash Wednesday Morning

Joel 2:12-19
2 Peter 1:2-11
St. Matthew 6:1-21

In the name of the Father and of the ✙ Son and of the Holy Spirit. Amen.

Tamar, daughter of David, put ashes on her head after being deceived and violated by her brother.

We put them on because we have been deceived and violated by our father the devil. He led us down terrible paths, promising things he could never give. Then after violating us, he filled us with shame at what we had done, at our small part, at our defiling. We are not clean. We will never again be what we once were. We dare not show our faces or look our mothers in the eye.

We mark ourselves with ashes to show our mourning, our shame, our death.

Mordecai and all the Jews put ashes on in response to the cruelty of the Persians.

We also have a cruel master. We have enslaved ourselves to sin, given in to passions and to good desires corrupted. They control us like animals, rutting in heat, without shame or knowledge.

Sin ruins the good things of God. It causes us to be dissatisfied with what He has given. We compare reality to popular sitcoms, romance novels, and adventure stories. We compare reality to television commercials, political rhetoric, and even theological rhetoric. Reality fails every time. Our lives pale in comparison to all our fantasies. Our friendships are not as lively as those on television. Our wives aren't as exciting as the characters in movies. Our careers are boring and sickly compared to the hype of human resources and recruiting. Not even our pastors are as profound, dedicated, or faithful as those on Issues, Etc.

We are emotionally flat, looking for joy, excitement, and entertainment. We refuse to believe that God may have called us to a dull existence on purpose, that dull is safe, and that there are joyous, good things all around us. We reject the good as not good enough, not exciting enough, too predictable and boring.

Repent. You are not too important to be bored.

Job sat among the ashes for his own sins. So did the king of Nineveh. Jeremiah says that we must cower in ashes. It is not just the devil's fault. We are victims, to be sure. But it is also our fault, our own fault, our own most grievous fault.

Yet God "lifts the needy from the ash heap" (Ps. 113:7), and He gives to those who mourn a garland instead of ashes (Isa. 61:3). He forgives the sins of the penitent. He clothes Adam and Eve. He re-establishes David's throne forever.

The opposite of covetousness is contentment. People who are content are thankful. The first step in turning yourself from sin is to name your sin, to confess it, to admit it. Part of that admission is that the sin is evil, that what you desire is evil, that you do not need it, are not served by it, and so forth.

The next step is thankfulness for what you have. We need to learn to confess that what the Lord has given is good. If He has made you single, God be praised, that is good. If He has provided a wife, that is good, God be praised. We need to search out and confess the good of His providence and give thanks for it. We confess not only our sin. We also confess the goodness of the Lord in His gifts.

This is the famous lesson of St. Francis in his sermon to the birds, so easily lost in the cuteness of the rhetoric. His point is that the goodness of the Lord is all around us in creation. Our response should not be dissatisfaction, but thanks and praise. Thanks and praise, an honest appraisal of the Lord's providence, creates joy and satisfaction and contentment. It is an attitude shift. Instead of trying to make your children be what you want them to be, you accept that the Lord has given them as gifts, and you marvel and delight in them. Instead of trying to bend your wife to your will, you rejoice in her faithfulness and loyalty, in her gentleness and piety. Instead of trying to get your own way, you submit and serve as one unworthy of the many good things in your life.

Your ashes are smeared today. There is no beauty in them. The world cannot see anything in them but an ugly smudge of dirt and death. But for those with the eyes of faith, they are in the form of a cross, that most lovely and dear of all symbols, that emblem of our hope.

We set our faces toward Jerusalem today. We turn our backs on sin. We look through the gallows on Golgotha and see the glory of the cross enlightening the empty tomb. He has been lifted up from the earth to draw us to Him, to drain the Law's accusing power, to empty hell's claim, to crush the devil's head, to bestow peace upon the meek.

You are a holy people, anointed with ashes. You belong to the Lord. His mark and name are upon you. This is what it is to be sanctified, to be holy. You are forgiven, to be sure, but there is more than that. You are not only forgiven, or just made even with God, as though you never did anything wrong, and that is that. There is more. For not only has your debt been wiped out, but there is credit in your account. You aren't just even; you are holy. You belong to Him. You have the superabundance of His good works counting as your own, and the earth, indeed all of the universe, is your inheritance.

So remember that you are dust and that you will return to dust. But remember also that God is a man, dust like you, joined to your temptations and sorrow, welded to your death, who was roasted to death in the Father's wrath, reduced to ashes, and laid to rest in God's good acre as a ransom, a whole burnt offering. That man is risen again from the dead and has come forth from the earth like a plant in the spring, that He would be your God. Turn your back on sin. Turn toward the Lord and His mercy. For here is peace and joy. Here is hope and faith.

Thus says the Psalmist, "The lines have fallen for me in pleasant places; indeed, I have a beautiful inheritance" (Ps. 16:6).

In ✠ Jesus' name. Amen.

Ash Wednesday Evening

Joel 2:12-19
2 Peter 1:2-11
St. Matthew 6:1-21

In the name of the Father and of the ✠ *Son and of the Holy Spirit. Amen.*

Throughout our Lord's ministry, but particularly in the Sermon on the Mount, our Lord denounces the false teaching and interpretation of Holy Scripture which had led people to refrain from sinning in an outward manner while their hearts remained completely corrupt and evil. It is not enough for God that men refrain from murdering one another. To be pure and holy, you must also not grow angry. It is not enough to not commit adultery. You must also refrain from all lust and impure thoughts.

The Law demands to be kept inwardly as well as outwardly—perfectly. All transgressions deserve punishment.

But now, in the same sermon, in what was read tonight, the Lord moves to outward things. Here is a great surprise: He is not condemning outward sins, like adultery and murder, nor secret sins of the heart, but He is condemning what seem to be good works. He is condemning charity, prayers, and fasting.

He does not denounce the works themselves, of course. He is not against charity, prayers, and fasting; rather, He denounces the purpose and aim of the Pharisees. In fact, what is so critical, exegetically, are the "thats." They are "thats" of purpose. The problem is not praying in the synagogue; the problem is praying in the synagogue THAT they would be seen praying. The works themselves might be good, but the Pharisees ruined them by their intentions. They were seeking not to serve their neighbors or to restrain their flesh but were instead seeking their own glory and honor before men.

Have we never done the same? That is a serious and dangerous question, for all such giving, prayers, and fasts, regardless of how great or abundant or expensive they may be, are useless and even damning.

Listen carefully. Our difficulty in hearing this lesson is legion. On the one hand, we are no different than they were. We are always looking over our shoulders to see who is watching. We are always adding up imaginary ledgers of what we've done and what is owed us. Have you never had a friend over for dinner and then expected the favor to be returned? Have you never had a friend over for dinner out of obligation because it was your turn? What if you always do the cooking and cleaning? Will you not grow annoyed that your friend never returns the favor? Have you never said "good morning" and expected a kind response? Have you never become disgusted and angry if you were friendly and said "hello," and the kindness wasn't returned?

Here is the harsh truth: In your fallen flesh, you think you are owed things. People ought to be polite to you. They ought to be nice to you. Your generosity ought to be noticed and praised. Why? Because you are polite and nice, and you deserve recognition.

Repent. What good is your politeness if you do it for a reward? But this is just the tip of the phylactery. We are no better than the Pharisees. We care deeply about our reputations, what people think of us. We crave recognition.

And on the other hand, we are even worse than the Pharisees. We have perverted this doctrine of inward purity and used it as an excuse to not act. We have denied the goodness of good works because of awareness. We have refused to discipline our bodies or minds and pasted on a false veneer of piety, pretending that we were waiting until the good works rose up out of us spontaneously, knowing full well, if we were honest, that they never would. St. Paul wrote that the Lord loves a cheerful giver, but we love our stuff. We haven't felt one hundred percent jolly in giving, so we've kept the money for ourselves and blamed God and our pretend piety for it.

This is a sore abuse. The Lord does not preach the Law to keep us from good works. He does not say that we should not fast because we cannot fast perfectly. Rather, He expects us to fast, even as He expects us to give to the poor. "When you give to the poor or fast," He says, "do not be like the hypocrites." He does not say, "If you choose to fast or love your neighbor, of your own free will, then be sure to do it better than the Pharisees." That is not what He says. He says, "*when* you do these things."

You will fast. Period. You will. You will know hardship in this life. If you do not do it voluntarily, if you do not take advantage of the time you have been given to train while you still have plenty, how will you fare when this hardship is forced upon you? The more we sweat in training, the less we bleed in war.

We cannot, and we do not, give alms, pray, or fast perfectly without any sin or selfish desire. That is true. Our fallen nature corrupts every good work. But we are to keep on trying anyway, not to earn God's favor or to impress men, but simply because this is what we were created to do, and we need the practice. God gives good gifts to men. We have been created in and restored to His image, so we also should give. We need to prepare for times of persecution and temptation. He bids us to follow Him to the cross, so we need to discipline our bodies and minds. We need to learn to trust that God's will is always best, that God is good.

And when we fail—whether it is by eating when we said we would not or eating what we said we wouldn't, or by lying, or by bragging, or by committing some sin—then we repent and try again. We do not stop. We repent and attempt again to amend our sinful lives. Do not stop doing good works because your works aren't perfect. Imperfect though they are, they are still good.

If you aren't a cheerful giver, keep on giving until you are. If you aren't a faithful faster, keep on trying until you are—which is to say, until you die, until you are delivered from this body of death and the infection of original sin. St. Paul uses the analogy of athletic training to describe the life of faith. We are learning. We are practicing. Of course, we're not perfect. The deadly error is either to think that we are perfect, that our works merit God's favor, or, just as deadly, to give up and think that God doesn't care.

It has been a common and pernicious confusion, in the Missouri Synod in particular, to think that good works aren't good if the doer becomes aware of them. That is false. It is true, in a sense, that our good works are corrupted by our fallen nature. They aren't perfectly pure. They don't merit God's favor. When we become aware of them, our pride gets involved. But it is not true that the corruption takes away their objective goodness. You might feed your daughter in the hope that she will love you for it, that you will be rewarded, or just that she will stop crying, but the food that you give her still does what it was meant to do. God provides for her through you, and that is good, even if you are not perfect in every way and knew you were just fulfilling your duty.

Your works are good. For even though you fail in part, even though you know there are rewards and honor and such, you are doing them in faith, as one of the baptized, one whose life and hands belong to God. You want to do good. You want to keep the Law. The works are good even as you are good—by promise. You are good. God Himself has said so, has promised it. You are washed in the blood of the Lamb as poured out in the Holy Supper. The name of God, who is good, has been placed upon you and upon the works of your hands. He declares you good, clean, pure, holy, for the sake of His Son. He gives you a part to play in His kingdom for your good and for your neighbor's good.

Therefore, we are called upon to repent, to change our ways, to reset our wills once again, to subdue the old man in us and leave behind our sins, which are a constant threat to our faith and to our loved ones. So also are we called to rejoice and bask in the goodness of God who does not give up on us just because we sin and fail. He is patient. He is generous. He is good and merciful. He does not quit. He loves us all the way to the end.

He invites you to pray because He is your true Father. You are His true child. He is good and declares you to be good. He who is eager and ready to forgive your sins even before you ask, and who provides daily bread, has delivered you from the evil one by His innocent suffering and death.

In ✠ Jesus' name. Amen.

Thursday after Ash Wednesday

Isaiah 38:1-6
St. Matthew 8:5-13

In the name of the Father and of the ✠ *Son and of the Holy Spirit. Amen.*

The Lord's authority does not require Him to heal the centurion's servant. He has the authority, not the obligation.

The centurion's appeal is not to authority, but for compassion. His servant is at the point of death and grievously tormented. To state the need is enough. He trusts the Lord will move in compassion and heal his servant. The centurion is explicit. He knows that he is not worthy, but he also knows that the Lord is merciful. He expects the Lord to act.

How does he know this? Because the Lord has said to him, "Come," and he has come. He has said to him, "Pray," and the centurion has prayed. The centurion has done what he has done, believed what he has believed, asked what he has asked, not under his own authority, but by divine command. Flesh and blood have not revealed this to him, but rather the Father in heaven.

It is a strange thing, then, that our Lord praises the man's faith. What credit did he deserve for that? His faith was not his own. It was not of his own making. It was a gift. Its strength sat not in the will or discipline or effort of the centurion, but rather according to the Lord's grace and mercy.

But that is the whole point. The centurion does get the credit. It is his faith because the Lord, in His mercy, has given it to him. This is the key doctrine of Christianity: The Father gives credit to us for works performed by the Son and blames the Son for our sin. So the Lord gives the centurion faith and then praises him for it. He commands that the centurion pray, then He answers.

What has the Lord commanded you to pray? Our Father. How then will He not hear? He will hear. He will answer. His name will be hallowed in you. His kingdom will come to you. His will will be done upon you. He will give you the bread you need for life. He will forgive your trespasses and create in you forgiveness for others. He will lead you out of temptation and deliver you from evil. He will give you these things and then give you credit for having them.

Why? Because He Himself is a man under authority who comes at His Father's command in order to capture humanity for heaven.

In ✠ *Jesus' name. Amen.*

FRIDAY AFTER ASH WEDNESDAY

Isaiah 58:1-9
St. Matthew 5:43-6:4

In the name of the Father and of the ✠ Son and of the Holy Spirit. Amen.

Be perfect as your Father is perfect" is the Sermon on the Mount's version of "Be holy because I the Lord your God am holy." What we are called to with these words is simply perfect obedience and love. Against this standard, who can stand?

The Father's perfection looks like indiscretion. He causes the sun and the rain to provide their benefits to the evil and the good, to the just and the unjust alike. But it isn't indiscretion. It is grace.

The Father bestows good things upon the earth out of His own goodness and without thought to either how they will be received or what His reward will be. He does not calculate. He does not keep a ledger. He is good. And so He showers the earth with goodness, with mercy, with grace. Nothing could be more God-like, more holy, more perfect than love of enemies.

To be sure, this whole thing is a Law passage. It tells us what to do, what to be, what the standard is. But the Law is God's will. In it He reveals Himself. He doesn't simply say, "Be perfect," and then walk away with His accusing gun smoking in the aftermath of our destruction. Rather, His accusing Law empties us in order to show us what His perfection and holiness is: He loves His enemies. That is to say that His perfection and holiness is that He loves those who break His Law. He provides for and is merciful to those who provide no advantage to Him, loving those who do not love Him. Thus does He send the blessing rain and the warming sunshine upon us, whether we are good or bad, just or unjust.

Again, the Father's perfection looks a lot like indiscretion, but it isn't. It is grace. The Lord Himself is the only one who can stand against this standard. The Son is perfect as the Father is perfect, fulfilling His own Law, perfect in obedience and love. Perhaps that is why this word "perfect" is the word He utters from the cross as His obedience and love come to completion. For the word here translated "perfect" is the final word from the cross, usually translated "finished."

In ✠ Jesus' name. Amen.

Saturday after Ash Wednesday

Isaiah 58:9-14
St. Mark 6:47-56

In the name of the Father and of the ✠ Son and of the Holy Spirit. Amen.

If the Lord were a spirit, we would have reason to be afraid. But He is a man, flesh of our flesh and bone of our bones. As Eve was taken out of her failure husband, so was the Lord taken out of Eve that Eve would be made perfect. He walks. He has callouses upon His feet. He is a man.

He is alone on the land, and He sees that His disciples are struggling against the wind. They struggle as well against the Holy Spirit, for they do not understand the miracle of the loaves. The waves are crashing against them. It is chaos like unto that over which the Spirit once hovered, and they are in danger. So our Lord walks with calloused feet across the stormy sea to the boat, and though He comes to intervene, to save them from a watery hell, they are afraid.

Their fear is misplaced, of course. He comes in mercy, with peace, to love.

It is the same for us. He climbs into our boat. He joins Himself to our cause. He is a man, one of us, a ransom and a sacrifice to satisfy the Spirit's demands and silence the devil once and for all.

He tells them to not be afraid. He will see them to the shore. The wind, the Holy Spirit, is no longer against them. Now He, who once was their enemy, gently blows them back to the promised land.

They do not understand. They did not understand the loaves, and the kingdom is centered in eating. Their hearts were hard, but the Lord persists in His patient love. He will go back and satisfy the chaos, meet the Law's demands and the punishment that justice requires. Like

Jonah, He will be sacrificed and rise again on the third day. Like Jonah, He will preach repentance and faith to the Gentiles, and mercy will follow ashes.

They do not understand, but they bring Him the sick. They do not understand, but they hang upon His words.

We do not understand either. We see in a mirror dimly. We are not greater or more sophisticated than the apostles. But let us bring our sick souls nonetheless to the place of feeding and healing, where the waves of chaos are stilled and sins are forgiven. For our God is a man, and we have an advocate with the Father, a friend in the Spirit.

In ✠ Jesus' name. Amen.

The First Sunday in Lent—Invocabit

Genesis 3:1-21
2 Corinthians 6:1-10
St. Matthew 4:1-11

In the name of the Father and of the ✠ Son and of the Holy Spirit. Amen.

As it was with Eve, so it was with the Lord. The first line of attack is eating. After air and water, this seems to be our most basic need and also the source of much pleasure and much abuse. The Lord had provided for His people with bread in the desert. He was, at that very moment, providing for the needs of humanity all over the world. Why should He go hungry? Why shouldn't He have what He provides for everyone else? How would it be a sin to take what is His if He is the Son of God?

It would have been a sin because the Holy Spirit took Him there to fast. The point of our Lord being the Son is not that He gets the inheritance, power, or rights, but that He is obedient to His Father. He waits for His Father to provide. He does not make His own way. He trusts that His Father will see Him through.

This is precisely what happens on the cross. The Father forsakes the Son. He leaves Him in hell, under the devil's torture and power. The Son becomes guilt, sin, a curse. But in the midst of it, even though He has been forsaken, He commits His spirit to His Father. He never loses faith. He never gives up hope. He is the perfect Son. He waits on the Father. He is obedient.

"It is written, 'Man shall not live by bread alone, but by every word that comes from the mouth of God.'"

Then the devil goes after our Lord's piety: "Prove that you trust God, that you believe in His Word." The devil quotes Scripture: "He will command his angels concerning you." The angels are there to serve. The Scriptures say that they will intervene for God's children. Why not show you believe it? Or why not show it to convince the devil that God's Word is true? If you are a child of God, won't the angels save you?

"Again it is written, 'You shall not put the Lord your God to the test.'"

Then the final appeal: "Bow down to me. Receive the glory and kingdoms of this world." This seems the most crass attempt and the most ridiculous. But it shows what all sin is. All sin is devil worship. All sin steals from God what is His.

"For it is written, 'You shall worship the Lord your God, and him only shall you serve.'"

All the temptations show us something of the character of sin and the character of the God who overcomes sin. But the Lord's response also shows us the best weapon we have against temptation and the only weapon we need. He says, again and again, "It is written."

The strategy of the devil against our first parents, and then against our Savior, was to plant doubt. He wants us to place ourselves into the role of judge. We will decide what is good for food, pleasing to the eye, and capable of making us wise. We will decide if He is worthy of being our God. This is what we do when we declare, "My God wouldn't do this or say that." But, in fact, we don't get to decide who God is or what He should do. He tells us who He is and what He does in His Word. Faith built on emotions and feelings or our own reason and goodness is like seed sown on rocky ground. It has no root. In time of temptation, it withers and dies.

The answer to doubt is God's Word. It is written. It is not fleeting, corruptible, or changing. It is solid, lasting, eternal. All things pass away, but the Word of God does not pass away. It is written, in the first place, on the page, not in our hearts. Even the Lord Himself, in the desert, submits to the written Word. It is the written, objective, unchanging Word.

That is why the first Law was written in tablets of stone. That is why Job longs for an iron pen and rock and molten lead, that he might engrave a hope that would last forever:

> For I know that my Redeemer lives, and at the last he will stand upon the earth. And after my skin has been thus destroyed, yet in my flesh I shall see God, whom I shall see for myself, and my eyes shall behold, and not another. My heart faints within me! (Job 19:25-27).

It is written. It is trustworthy. It cannot be changed or forgotten. It endures. Thus written—and not subject to the wavering and episodic feelings and opinions of men—it is the sword of the Spirit, and the Spirit does war with the devil.

But for all of that, we don't face the devil the same way that our Lord did. We can't. We are always complicit in temptation because of the sin that infects us. The Lord can hear the temptation and not sin. He doesn't have any desire for evil. He doesn't imagine it. He simply rejects it because it is outside the Word of God.

But when we hear temptation—no matter how vile, stupid, or evil it is—there is part of us that participates. We consider it. We imagine it. And we are dirtied by it, corrupted, and then confused. We do not know what it is to be hungry and to not consider food because the Father hasn't given it. Our passions place thoughts into our heads directly. We are not in control. We are not strong. We do not really resist.

Repent.

We can only be saved by grace. Thanks be to God, He is gracious. For all our complicity with Satan, for all our vile selfishness and perversions, we have a great strength: The Lord is a man and is on our side.

Everything that Jesus did, He did for us, in our place, as our substitute and champion. Everything. He did nothing that wasn't for us.

So also the temptation. He faced down the devil. He endured those trials for our sake, so that we would not have to, so that we would not be held accountable for our sins, so that the devil could not have us.

The temptation of Jesus shows us the right way to respond to temptation: with fasting, that is bodily discipline; prayer; and the Word of God. He is an example, the most excellent and perfect example, of a truly godly and God-pleasing life. But more than that—and here is what almost nobody gets—the temptation of Jesus stands in our place. We don't have to overcome the devil. We don't have to suffer for our sins. We don't even have to die. The Holy Spirit did this to Jesus on purpose, in our stead, for us, so that we would be spared. This is what pleases the Father. This is what He was anointed for by St. John in the Jordan's filthy water. We are the prize that Jesus desires, His inheritance, the plunder of hell, a bride worthy of God Himself.

Once again: We don't have to overcome the devil. We don't have to suffer for our sins. We don't even have to die. That is what Jesus has done for us. He was tempted for us even as He was crucified for us.

One more thing to note: Eve fell by eating. Jesus resisted taking food from the devil in the desert. And He redeems us by feeding. The same action that plunged the world back to near chaos, that which He denied Himself, now unites and reconciles God's children to God. His body and His blood are better than manna in the desert. Here is balm for your wounds, courage for your fight, peace for your soul, and the strength you need to face temptation. Here is the Word of God written in stone in the flesh of Mary, hidden in bread, that you would not stand against the accuser but would live as God's own holy child.

In ✠ Jesus' name. Amen.

Monday of Invocabit

Ezekiel 34:1-16
St. Matthew 25:31-46

In the name of the Father and of the ✠ Son and of the Holy Spirit. Amen.

Just when our Lord is about to stand trial, He declares that a day is coming when He will judge all people. He is the Shepherd who separates His sheep from the devil's goats.

Those who think they should be judged by their works will be. Here are the damning words: "Lord, when did we see you hungry or thirsty or a stranger or naked or sick or in prison, and did not minister to you?" Ask for a list of failures, insist that you have done what you should, and you will get it—and not just what you deserve, but what you want. Everyone gets the lord he wants. If you want a lord of justice, a tooth for a tooth and an eye for an eye, if you want an accounting and comparison to the rest of the world, you will get it and you will be damned.

This is one of the clearest bits of evidence in the New Testament that there is a dark side to the Holy Gospel. Those who receive the blessing of Christ in faith, who claim to have done nothing, saying, "Lord, when did we see you hungry and feed you, or thirsty and give you drink?" receive credit for good works they did not perform and don't remember. They remain with Jesus and go to heaven. They are His sheep by grace. But those who argue that they've done enough, who insist on being judged by their works, will reap what they have sown and be thrown into the everlasting fire prepared for the devil and his angels.

Repent.

When did you ever do anything? Change the question. Do not be afraid. Look up and ask, "When did Christ do something?" That is the question that leads to life. Don't look to your works. Look to His. The Christ went to trial and was condemned by Pilate. The ironic title "King of the Jews" was placed over His head, ironic because it was a false charge, but completely true. There He paid for sins that He did not commit, and which we don't even remember, and now even He has forgotten them. He has been condemned and has died that you might get credit for works you did not perform. Turn from "When did we fail?" to "When, O Lord, did You serve us?" And then, "Where, O Lord, do You serve us?" For He lives. And He serves in His Word and Holy Supper.

In ✠ Jesus' name. Amen.

Tuesday of Invocabit

Isaiah 55:6-11
St. Matthew 21:10-17

In the name of the Father and of the ✠ Son and of the Holy Spirit. Amen.

The crowds in Jerusalem welcomed our Lord with great enthusiasm. The city shook at His coming. The word here is our word "seismic." Jerusalem was shaken as though an earthquake had struck.

But their answer to the question, "Who is this?" was "This is the prophet Jesus, from Nazareth of Galilee."

They shook for naught. As pious as their answer might sound, it shows their willful ignorance of the actual prophets. At the very least, they should have met Him as a king:

> Rejoice greatly, O daughter of Zion!
>   Shout aloud, O daughter of Jerusalem!
> Behold, your king is coming to you;
>   righteous and having salvation is he,
> Humble and mounted on a donkey,
>   on a colt, the foal of a donkey. (Zech. 9:9)

Despite their willful ignorance and disobedience, nothing would stop the actual earthquake that would strike Jerusalem that coming Friday. Creation shook with real violence as the Father and the Spirit restored creation through the death of the Son. The earth shook the court of the Gentiles open. The earth shook sight and healing into the blind and lame, that children might sing Hosanna, unencumbered or hindered, with perfect praise.

To say that Jesus is a rabbi or a prophet or even a king is not enough. Zechariah's words prophesy that this king is not like earthly kings. He comes in humility and without oppression. He does not tax. He does not press our sons into foreign wars for expansion and profit. He does not lie. He rules by dying, by forgiving, by rising, by feeding.

He is King Messiah, anointed to be the sacrifice of salvation, the priestly victim whose humility will send Him to hell on a cross that we might be redeemed and reconciled to God—cleansed, pure, and holy by divine mercy and grace. To praise Him with anything less than worship, to fail to see that He is the God of Abraham, Isaac, and Jacob is to reject Him for gods of our own design.

Poor Jerusalem. Poor America. We don't know what is good for us because we don't know the One who is good. May God in His mercy spare us and deliver us from this body of death, not because we deserve it, but because that is who He is and what He does.

In ✠ Jesus' name. Amen.

Ember Wednesday in Lent

1 Kings 19:3-8
St. Matthew 12:38-50

In the name of the Father and of the ✠ Son and of the Holy Spirit. Amen.

"This generation" certainly applied to the men and women of our Lord's day. They should have known better than the Ninevites and the Queen of Sheba. They had Moses and the prophets. But they rejected the Messiah in willful obstinacy. Moses and the prophets were loved for their poetry and beauty apart from their content.

"This generation" also applies to us. For "this generation" is ever current. In the context of the New Testament, the term means something like "people who live for themselves" or "people caught up in their own world and concerns, in their own day, apart from the prophets and God's Word."

In that sense, every generation is "this generation." The emphasis is on "this." They are people defined by themselves instead of being defined by God.

Listen to these passages from Luke:

"This generation is an evil generation. It seeks for a sign, but no sign will be given to it except the sign of Jonah" (Luke 11:29).

"[T]he blood of all the prophets, shed from the foundation of the world, may be charged against this generation" (Luke 11:50).

The Son of Man "must suffer many things and be rejected by this generation" (Luke 17:25).

"Truly, I say to you, this generation will not pass away until all has taken place" (Luke 21:32).

Those statements are all true of the Jews. They are also true of us. We are an evil generation, generated in the sin of our fathers. Repent. We have been focused on ourselves and our own times, thinking ourselves wiser than our fathers, unnaturally bent on our present and future.

The Ninevites are surprising examples. They are not of "this generation" but have been generated of the Lord, born from above, even if Jonah in his prejudice didn't want them to be. Flesh and blood did not reveal the Lord to them—no, not Jonah—but the Father in heaven revealed Himself to them, albeit through the reluctant prophet.

There is something in this account of the wickedness of Gentiles and the steadfast mercy of God that loves even them. The Ninevites aren't wonderful people, but they are loved by God. At His Word, they repent and are spared. There is also something in this of the stubbornness and frailty of those called to preach who think they know best how and when and where to preach.

The Queen of Sheba also gets credit for being a discerning hearer of God's Word despite her ethnicity and many crimes. By God's grace, she was able to recognize the wisdom of the Lord in Solomon, son of David. She shows us the way.

While this is meant to shame the Jews, who should have known better, we should not miss the invitation the Lord is making to them. If there is room in the kingdom for the Ninevites and citizens of Sheba, there is certainly room for stupid Pharisees and reluctant, fearful Jews. And if there is room for them, then there is also room for us.

The term "generation" does get redeemed to some degree. For now, presently, in this time, all generations, even this generation, call St. Mary blessed.

Jesus is risen from the dead. He redeems "this generation." He comes preaching not just the repentance of Jonah and the acceptance of

Gentiles but also the real year of jubilee. All slavery, debt, and sins are forgotten. The curse of Babel and the distinction of Abraham—that is, the distinction between Sarah and Hagar, between Jews and Gentiles— are undone. The Holy Spirit has come. We have a new Adam, a new Father, and are made His holy people. We are generated from above.

In ✠ Jesus' name. Amen.

Thursday of Invocabit

Ezekiel 18:1-9
St. Matthew 15:21-28

In the name of the Father and of the ✠ Son and of the Holy Spirit. Amen.

I t is not right to give the children's bread to the dogs.

But this woman is bold. Her response to being ignored is to keep on asking. Her response to overhearing that He came only for the lost sheep of the house of Israel is to fall down and worship Him. Her prayer for her daughter's demon possession has been distilled down to simply, "Lord, help me."

Then He says, "It is not right to take the children's bread and throw it to the dogs."

But she is bold. She does not quit. She has the promises. She is a Gentile, but she has hope. She has the Word. She waits on the Lord. She waits for Him to show His mercy. She does not want the children's bread. She wants more. She wants His bread. She wants Him.

"Yes, Lord," she says, "yet even the dogs eat the crumbs that fall from their masters' table."

Put me in your lap, Lord. Scratch behind my ear. Throw the ball. And let me eat what falls from the loaf of which you eat.

Better to be a doorkeeper in the house of God than to dwell in the tents of wickedness. Better to be a dog in the home of the Lord than to be the play-thing of demons.

Some would say that we should not see in this bread anything of the Holy Communion. They tell us that every instance of bread or wine in the Scripture is not a sacrament, does not bestow the forgiveness of sins, is not the body and blood of Jesus. Sometimes, they say, bread is just bread.

But I wonder if that is ever so. Is bread, from the perspective of heaven, ever *just* bread? Does God ever feed us, provide for all that we need to support this body and life in a casual, even accidental, way? Is there any providence from heaven, any feeding, any love or mercy of God apart from the body and blood of Jesus Christ crucified and raised?

No. Everything goes back to the cross. The Holy Communion brings the cross back to us. The Holy Communion is everything.

But this isn't the feeding of the five thousand or turning water into wine. There is no actual bread here even as there are no actual dogs. These things are metaphors. They stand for other things. There is only the Lord, His disciples, the woman, her daughter, and the demons. The demons are not metaphors. They are real. So are the daughter, sorely vexed, and the mother, full of fear. Jesus is not a metaphor either, nor are His disciples. They are real. They are there. And everyone there, except Jesus, is helpless and at His mercy.

This is His intent. He is the fulfillment of all the prophecies and types, of all the hopes and dreams of Israel, the culmination that all creation longs for. His intent is that His ministers would pray and that His people would pray. His intent is that they would come to Him with the boldness and confidence of dear children asking their dear father. In this, the woman puts the apostles to shame. She is bolder than they. She is confident. She wants not the children's bread. She wants to share in His bread, the Lord's bread. Could that be only a metaphor for help and nothing more?

Surely she wants *more* than bread, but does that mean she *doesn't* want bread? I don't think so. What she wants, whether she can fully articulate it or not, is fellowship with Jesus. She wants to be divorced from demons and married to Christ. She wants to leave them behind and sit at table with Jesus. In any case, her prayer has gone from, "Have mercy on me for my daughter is possessed by a demon" to "Help me" to "Share Your bread with me."

Could that be eucharistic? That is, in asking for bread, even if it is mainly a metaphor, is she actually asking for what our Lord gives in the Lord's Supper? The Lord's Supper is not a metaphor or symbol. The bread we break is His holy body given to us to eat. It is not simply a reminder or a ceremony. In it our Lord gives us His risen body and medicine against sin, protection from demons. Doesn't her plea for bread have something to do with how the Lord helps us, has mercy upon us, delivers us and our children from demons? Yes.

But here, above all, is why this is eucharistic: The Lord is constant and unchanging. He did not one day decide to try something new and invent the Holy Sacraments. This is how He always is and always interacts with His people. He feeds. The sacrifices were mainly meat for eating. The manna in the desert was also food. Yet man lives not by bread alone, even by manna alone, but by every Word that proceeds from the mouth of God, even as our Lord reminded the devil last week. So the Lord does more than feed the body. He provides for the soul through the body. You can't wash a soul. So you wash the body with water in the Triune name of God, and the soul is thereby washed. We call that baptism. You can't touch the soul or feed it apart from the body. So Jesus feeds our bodies with spiritual food, with what the soul needs to be strengthened and cleansed. He does not sit in heaven and think nice things toward us. He actually enters into creation. He speaks through human words, in a human voice. He feeds us when bread and wine become His body and blood, even as He washes us with water.

Food is not a metaphor. It is real. So is God's grace. God's Word has taken up flesh to be our Savior, to walk among us, to suffer as us, to be punished and killed in our place. He has accomplished what He was sent to do. He has pulled us out of hell. And that we would have communion with Him, He enters into us by way of the mouth, feeds us with Himself and thereby consumes us, makes us a part of Him, while taking residence in us. It is not the children's bread He gives. That would not be right for us, mere dogs, Gentiles. But He gives us more. He gives out of His affection and generosity. He gives Himself, the bread come down from heaven, the bread of life.

He hears the woman's prayer. He gives Himself to her. The demons depart, banished. He hears your prayer as well. He gives Himself to you in His bread. The demons cannot have you. You are His.

In ✠ Jesus' name. Amen.

Ember Friday in Lent

Ezekiel 18:20-28
St. John 5:1-15

In the name of the Father and of the ✠ Son and of the Holy Spirit. Amen.

This Bethesda business is disturbing. It seems to come from nowhere. There is no record of this pool or its healing properties anywhere but here in St. John's Gospel.

But it is worse than that. This is a strange and seemingly cruel angel. He lifts the hopes of so many but only rewards the least sick or those who are wealthy or connected enough to get someone to carry their beds. What a sad plight, to sit by a pool where healing is offered but to be unable to obtain it because of weakness or poverty.

The Jews had a legend of another pool where an evil spirit lived. Could it be that this angel who disturbs the waters at Bethesda was an evil angel? Perhaps this angel is bent on disturbing the souls of men and leading them to despair. Perhaps. For this pool, with an angel who only helps the least sick or wealthy, is no prefiguring of Holy Baptism and God's grace. This does seem to fit with the satanic lies of a god being cruel, being random and inconsistent, or only loving the wealthy.

It could also be that the five porches here are meant to remind us of the five books of Moses. As we heard in Ezekiel, there is a kind of promise in the Law. If you are perfect, you will live. But no matter how good you are, how perfect, a single sin will destroy it all. When a righteous man turneth from righteousness, all his righteous deeds are forgotten. He that sinneth, shall die in his sins. Ezekiel shows us our need for a Savior, for the Messiah, because we cannot meet the Law's demands. The cruel angel shows our need as well.

The Lord's healing is not like the angel's healing. It is not based on merit or strength. Rather, the Lord provides for a man who cannot help himself.

His miracle also undoes the Sabbath. That is the point of the question "Wilt thou be made whole?" He knows the man wants to be healed. That is why he is lying there. What He is asking is if the man wants to be sound throughout. If so, even though it is the Sabbath and evil rabbis have made up rules and will judge him for it, he is to take up his bed and walk. He is to turn his back on the rabbis and the pool.

Soundness, or wholeness, is not simply physical healing. The Lord asks for more. He seeks in the sick man the ability to discern the Word and will of God in distinction from the rules of men and the devil. Is it God's will to heal only those who can help themselves? Is it God's will that men serve the Sabbath or that the Sabbath serve men? Is it God's will to be merciful, or is He harsh and cruel? The man is told to walk away from the temptation to seek healing apart from grace.

Still, there is another problem. It seems as though the man did not quite have faith in the Christ. He does not know the name of Jesus, the One who healed him. To his credit, however, he knows enough to carry his bed and ignore the rabbis. After he encounters Christ in the temple—no coincidence that he encounters the Christ *in the temple*— he goes straightway to tell the Jews that it is Jesus who has made him whole. He knows, of course, that at best he will be ridiculed for this, and at worst, he might be stoned.

But what is that to him? He is whole. He is sound throughout. He has Christ and Christ by name: Jesus, the Lord who saves. He is free. Neither rabbis, soldiers, nor evil angels can harm him. He could not help himself, but the Lord helped him.

May God in His mercy make us all equally sound and whole.

In ✠ Jesus' name. Amen.

Ember Saturday in Lent

1 Thessalonians 5:14-23
St. Matthew 17:1-9

In the name of the Father and of the ✠ Son and of the Holy Spirit. Amen.

They were not afraid when they saw the divine nature showing through the man Jesus. They were not afraid when His face shone like the sun. They were not afraid when they saw Him talking with Moses and Elijah. That, they thought, was great. They loved it. They wanted to stay.

But then came the bright cloud and the command. And then they were terrified.

They heard of wars and armies, lightning and dragons, betrayal and conspiracies. They heard of violence and murder, injustice and hatred, of men's hearts failing them for fear. And they heard of death, for Moses and Elijah were talking with our Lord about His exodus: His horrifying death and abandonment by the Father.

That scared them. That began wisdom, for the fear of the Lord—not joy, not peace, not love, not hope, but the fear of the Lord—is the beginning of wisdom.

He responded to their fear not with a rebuke, but with mercy. He came to them. He touched them. He said to them, "Arise, and do not be afraid." And then, hearing Jesus, they saw only Jesus. Faith comes by hearing.

Where is the bright cloud of the Father? Where are Moses and Elijah? They are there. But in hearing Jesus, they saw only Jesus. Gone was all talk of staying on the mountain. Like Moses and Elijah, they had become converts. They recognized the goodness of the Lord in the sacrifice of the Son. They no longer chafed under the harshness of the

Law and its seemingly petty rituals. Hearing Jesus, they saw that all of it was to establish the means whereby men could be cleansed and re-enter fellowship with the Creator.

If the Lord goes to Jerusalem to die, if He suffers and bears wounds innocently, if He satisfies the Law and is banished to hell, it is good. For the Lord is good and His mercy endures forever. Let us rejoice in the vision and shrink not from the gift of the Father, our own ransom and hope, and therein apply our hearts to wisdom.

In ✠ Jesus' name. Amen.

The Second Sunday in Lent—Reminiscere

Genesis 32:22-32
1 Thessalonians 4:1-7
St. Matthew 15:21-28

In the name of the Father and of the ✠ Son and of the Holy Spirit. Amen.

Where is her husband? Every daughter has a father. Where is he?

The woman comes alone—no husband, no mother, no sister, no friend. She comes alone and seeks the Messiah's help. "Have mercy on me, O Lord, Son of David; my daughter is severely oppressed by a demon."

He answers her not a word.

What has her husband said? Has he been silent also? Does he blame her or the daughter for the demon oppression? Or does he blame himself? Is he ashamed of them, or is he afraid? Where are her mother, her sisters, her friends?

Perhaps she was bold in her first cries, but she is soon put in her place. Not only has she come alone, but also the Lord ignores her. He answers not a word. He walks on by.

The apostles become embarrassed, though it is hard to tell why. Are they embarrassed by her because she keeps crying out and is a nuisance to their comfort, like television ads for starving children? Or are they embarrassed because our Lord is not acting in a way they deem proper? Are they confused by His silence and what appears to be a lack of compassion? Do they want Him to show His power, to prove He is the Messiah and help her? Or do they just want to try and forget about the injustices of this world for a while?

Whatever the reason, they intervene, begging the Lord to send her away. But the Lord answers the woman, saying, "I was sent only to the lost sheep of the house of Israel."

Now it has gotten worse. She addresses Him as though she were one of the sheep. She calls Him "Lord, Son of David," but she is a Gentile. Her husband, if she has one, is not with her. This is a bit like me calling Oddie Ridley "Mama."† Perhaps I could get away with it, but it would be awkward. It is a title of intimacy and affection that, however much I might love her and she me, has not been given to me. I am not blood.

So what is her response to this awkward slam against her presumption? Does she slink away and hope people will forget about it? No, she comes and worships Him. It is sometimes translated as "kneel," but it actually means to fall on one's face, to lie down on the ground, fully submissive. She is a beggar, a penitent before her king, and she will not be driven off simply because she is not worthy.

Now she says simply, "Lord, help me." She drops all elaboration, all rationale, all plans for how He might be merciful, what He might do, and all claims on Him. Now it is only, "Help me," more clearly a cry for mercy than when she used the word mercy.

To which He says, "It is not right to take the children's bread and throw it to the dogs."

This insult is softened a bit by His use of the diminutive. He does say, in fact, "little dogs," and He might well mean "lap dogs" or "house dogs," something like that which a trendy socialite carries around in her purse. But even so, it is an insult nonetheless. Lacking the presence of her husband, it could be taken to mean something far worse: a dog who lets men use her for money. The implication is that she is unclean and unthinking. She throws herself down in front of Him with the same desperation that causes dogs to run to vomit or dung as well as

---

† Oddie Ridley is the beloved matriarch of a family at Redeemer.

48

to meat, greedily and without discernment. Who else has she thrown herself down in front of? How did this demon come into their lives in the first place?

Demons rarely come uninvited. We dangle our fingers in shark-infested waters with every sin. To open the internet to a porn site is to open a portal for the demons to come into your home. The internet never forgets. Neither do the demons. To harden your conscience so that you can enjoy your sin and then repent later is to invite them in as well. There are no victimless crimes, no small sins without consequences. What do we think of those who don't properly store their guns or dangerous chemicals in the presence of children? We are worse. Repent. We engage in dangerous activities. Not only our own lives but also the lives of our daughters, our sons, our spouses, and our loved ones are at stake.

The Canaanite woman must know the history of Jacob and how he wrestled all night with God. She also knows her own unworthiness to not only look at God but to touch Him or demand things of Him. "Yes, Lord," she says, and then she shows a fortitude and patience as great as Jacob's, but with keener insight. She is more humble than Jacob and also more cognizant of the promises.

No, she is not a sheep of Israel. That was presumptuous. She is not one of the children, but she does belong in the house. She wants not the children's bread. She wants the master's bread, and that belongs to His pets as well as to His children. She is not a sheep or a child, but neither is she a pig or some wild animal. She belongs in the house. He is her master. He marvels at and rewards her faith. Her daughter is healed. Let us marvel as well.

The circumstances of the affliction or the location of her husband don't matter. She needed a Messiah, a Savior, an advocate with the Father and a ransom for the devil, someone who would send the demons away and provide the bread that gives life. She knew where to look for all of that. She found Him, Jesus of Nazareth, and she recognized

Him more clearly than the apostles or any in Israel. She held God to His promises more fervently than Jacob. She contended with God and with Satan and overcame.

You have played with fire in your own life. You have put your marriage and family at risk with gossip, alcohol, pornography, gambling, and a whole host of lies. You have demanded they serve you; you have forgotten you were called to serve them. If the demons do not yet sorely oppress you and your children, they are nipping at your heels.

Repent. Throw yourself upon the mercy of Christ. Not only can He save you, but He has. He has taken your sins upon Himself. He has suffered the punishment you deserved, in your place, as your scapegoat. He has declared you righteous and placed His name upon you. He will hold you to His promises.

For in Him, you are not a Gentile, nor are you a dog. You are His bride. You are His chosen one declared immaculate and radiant, worthy of His love. So you can call Him "Son of David," or "Lord" or "God" or "King Messiah," but you are His intimate companion, the apple of His eye and affection. Though He is your king, you can call Him "Jesus."

And He gives you more than bread for children, more than cake for guests. He gives you His risen body and blood, Himself, in the Sacrament, to cure and heal your soul and to send the demons away. And this is more than just eating, more than strength for the day and a cure for what ails you; it is a penetration, the holy, intimate bond of husband and wife.

I suspect, in the end, that even if the Canaanite woman's husband were standing right there the whole time, that is why he isn't mentioned. For Jesus is her true husband.

In ✠ Jesus' name. Amen.

Monday of Reminiscere

Daniel 9:15-19
St. John 8:21-29

In the name of the Father and of the ✠ Son and of the Holy Spirit. Amen.

There are some translation problems in the King James rendering of John 8. The chief is adding a predicate to the great I AM. Our Lord says to them, "If ye believe not that I AM you will die in your sins." And again He says, "When you have lifted up the Son of Man you will know that I AM." The King James adds the "he." It renders both as "I am he" rather than simply "I AM." That "he" shifts the meaning slightly. It makes this a Messianic claim, but not a divine claim.

The problem is that the shift misses the offense—both what offended them and what offends us. They were confused in their fallen flesh about who and what the Messiah was to be. So are we. Here is the truth: Yahweh, the Creator, the only God, the One present in the burning bush is a man, and an ugly, dying, weak man at that.

Some years ago I was at a Lutheran school wrestling meet. Almost all of the schools there had wrestlers wearing sweatshirts with Bible passages on them. Their choices of passages were telling. No one had "Turn the other cheek" or "Do unto others as you would have done unto you" or "He who lives by the sword will die by the sword." No, instead, they all pulled passages out of context and turned them into something very similar to what you'd see on a Nike or Red Bull commercial, as though the victory of Christ and the promises He makes to His saints are about doing one's personal best and beating other people, rather than bearing a cross, being despised by the world, and dying.

The most offensive, however, was not a Bible passage at all. It was a shirt that said, "Jesus didn't tap." Tapping in this context isn't talking about Greco-Roman wrestling, but costumed television wrestling. There the loser taps the mat as a plea for mercy, in admission of defeat, as the victor cruelly and painfully twists his arm and pushes his face into the mat. To say "Jesus didn't tap" was meant to say that Jesus didn't give up. He kept fighting and, in a melodramatic surprise, flipped the situation and pinned the bad guy. Therefore you, too, should be like Jesus and not give up but flip it around and pin the devil.

That is off in several ways. It is true, in a sense, that Jesus didn't quit. But He was absolutely everything that we despise. He wasn't tough or strong. He didn't overcome the devil by strength as men count strength. He wasn't clever or impressive. He was disgusting, stricken, smitten, and afflicted. He was weak, beaten, defeated, dying. And when He is lifted up from the earth—in all the gore and pain, in all the things that we don't aspire to be or want to be—there we see our God: the great I AM of Abraham, Isaac, and Jacob—humiliated, defeated, dead.

There is a strength in that, a strength beyond the greatest athletes and soldiers the world has ever known, but it is not a strength that can be recognized except by faith. It is not counted as strength by men or by demons. For it is not a strength that can be turned to our advantage over others or even over ourselves. Jesus is no Rocky Balboa, pulling Himself up by the bootstraps. He is a worm and no man. He doesn't make for good bumper stickers or t-shirt slogans.

Repent. We have lusted after a god more fit for action films than for salvation. We have been ashamed of Him and tried to fashion Him into our own image.

Despite that, HE IS. He is the Great Being, the One Who Is, the I AM. You will not die in your sins because, shameful though it is, He has become a man to die for you. He has been humiliated, stricken, smitten, afflicted, and abandoned by His Father so that you would be spared. You will not go to Gehenna. He has already been there for you.

Look. There, upon the cross. See what He has become, what He Who Is has done and what He has undone for you.

There is some irony in the snide remark made by the Pharisees about Jesus killing Himself. He is both priest and victim. He does lay down His own life. But those men were not worthy to speak of such things. Neither are we. Still, He loved them, and He loved us, and He still loves us. And He gives us these things to contemplate, even freedom and boldness to dare to speak of them. And in that sense, He is the most beautiful and the most victorious at His ugliest and weakest, at His death on the cross.

May He, in His mercy, ever keep these mysteries before us.

In ✠ Jesus' name. Amen.

Tuesday of Reminiscere

1 Kings 17:8-16
St. Matthew 23:1-12

In the name of the Father and of the ✣ Son and of the Holy Spirit. Amen.

The discourse just read from Matthew took place in the temple on Palm Sunday. It immediately precedes the woes to the scribes and Pharisees. In it our Lord upholds the idea of an office being divine even when the men who fill it are evil. Then He warns against the hypocrisy that is born from love of honor which threatens all believers. Next, He reminds us that our true Father is our Father in heaven, His Father and our Father, even as He is our true teacher and master.

The command to "call no man your father" is obviously hyperbole. No serious Christian has ever refrained from calling his biological father by some sort of title that means, in essence, "Father." Nor has any Christian father forbidden his children from calling him "Father" or "Dad" or "Papa."

What, then, does our Lord command? He commands, in the first place, that we follow those who sit in the seat of Moses. This is about divine offices. When we address any man as teacher, master, father, shepherd, or helper, we do so seeing that these men are serving in offices that God has established and wherein He provides for us. We have earthly fathers and we have earthly teachers, but they are not our true fathers or our true teachers. Yet they are the means by which our true Father and teacher provides for us. Thus, we honor the office and obey.

So also, when we ourselves fill these offices, we should do so with humility, realizing that our children, employees, neighbors, and the like belong not to us but to our Father in heaven who made them. They are not ours to use. They do not exist for our honor or enjoyment, but for His.

The discourse concludes with these words: "And whosoever shall exalt himself shall be abased; and he that shall humble himself shall be exalted" (KJV).

All the ways that God serves and provides for us in this life—through fathers, pastors, teachers, and the like—serve to bring us to the ultimate office: the Messiah. It is our Lord Jesus Christ, who is abased and humbled for us on the cross and who is then glorified by the Father in the resurrection. He does what no rabbi could do. He lifts the burdens placed by Moses from our shoulders and places it upon His own. His works were not done to be seen by men, but by His Father the righteous judge. Now the Law is fulfilled. Now the accusations are removed. For Christ, our master and Lord, our teacher and Father, our brother and husband, has become the least of us, our servant, to make us His.

His yoke is easy, and His burden is light.

In ✠ Jesus' name. Amen.

WEDNESDAY OF REMINISCERE

Esther 13:8-11, 15-17
St. Matthew 20:17-28

In the name of the Father and of the ✠ Son and of the Holy Spirit. Amen.

This is our Lord's third prediction of His holy passion. He will be betrayed, killed, and He will rise again. He gave much the same prediction here as He had given after St. Peter's great confession and again after the transfiguration. But here He adds a detail: It will be death by crucifixion. Perhaps they might have guessed this since He had told them He would be handed to the Gentiles, or they might have guessed it from His command to the disciples that they must take the cross and follow Him, or they might have even seen it in His prophecy to Nicodemus that He would be lifted up from the earth like the bronze serpent. But it seems most likely that they did not quite get it and that this must have been a bit shocking, that the Lord would not only persist in His path toward sacrifice, but that He would be sacrificed in the most horrific, ignoble, and shameful way imaginable. His death itself is unclean.

The cross looms large before the Lord. He knows what is coming. He is ready, and He faces it calmly. His calmness comes from His faith in the Father's goodness and in the resurrection and also from His determination to save the disciples and all humanity.

That the disciples were surprised by the resurrection seems surprising to us. So also, we are surprised that James and John seem so blind to the character of the kingdom. But we often think that they had advantages that we don't, when, in fact, it is the other way around; we have advantages they didn't. We know the end of the story. We have the benefit of their ministry and writing and 2000 years of church history since Pentecost to help us with these things. We are dwarves standing on the shoulders of giants, and we are surprised that the giants don't see as far as we do.

The disciples should be admired all the more for their honesty and for unapologetically portraying their own foolishness and evil. They can do so because, post-resurrection and post-Pentecost, they are confident in the forgiveness and grace of Christ. So they lay it all out without apology, exposing their pride and ambition and also recording the rebuke: "Whoever would be great among you must be your servant, and whoever would be first among you must be your slave."

In this matter, as in all the Law, the Lord Himself is the supreme example, and the apostles follow closely. They serve us in being our fools and recording their sins, that we might have the benefit of their experience without the danger they endured. What a gracious and benevolent God is the Christ to serve us so. He has come to be our ransom.

Thus, the account ends much as it began. The Lord Christ goes on to be a sacrifice and to win the world for Himself.

In ✠ Jesus' name. Amen.

Thursday of Reminiscere

Jeremiah 17:5-10
St. Luke 16:19-31

In the name of the Father and of the ✠ Son and of the Holy Spirit. Amen.

The desire of the rich man for someone to be a messenger from the dead and warn his brothers and also the fact that the only one ever named who was raised from the dead is Lazarus is hard to find a mere coincidence. Of course, Lazarus, brother of Mary and Martha, was not a mere messenger of the dead but is, in fact, risen out of death. But far from leading to repentance, the resurrection of Lazarus triggers the hatred of the Pharisees so that they then begin to plot how to entrap and kill the Lord.

Abraham was right. Miracles don't create faith. Faith comes by hearing and hearing by the Word of God. If they will not hear Moses and the prophets, then even if someone like Lazarus rose out of death, they will not believe.

Some have tried to read this parable as Christ being the beggar Lazarus, for Christ was denied a place at His Father's table and balm for His wounds. Christ gives His life-blood to Gentile dogs. This reading is a stretch, but if such a suggestion causes us to meditate upon the mercy and grace of Christ in His death, resurrection, and Holy Supper, then it does the Lord's work.

What is abundantly clear is that Jesus is the God of Abraham, witnessed to and proclaimed in Moses and the prophets. He is the God of mercy, the one who appeared rich in the parable, clothed in purple and eating sumptuously every day. He was poor and damned, and this One who looked disgusting and ignoble was God's own beloved child.

There is more here, however, than simply the truism that we shouldn't judge a book by its cover. The richness of Lazarus comes precisely from his poverty. He has nothing. He is a beggar. Thus, there is plenty of room in him for what God gives through grace. As Luther famously said, we come to God with an empty sack, and He fills it with good things. The rich man is full and has no need of mercy. There is no place in him for what God would give, so he has only what is his. He gets what he deserves, and even in hell he is arrogant and thinks not only that he can still boss Lazarus around but that he is more clever in religious matters than Abraham. Even in hell, the rich man is still full of himself. And that, sadly, is the ultimate torment and sadness.

The mention of dogs closely allied with mercy and of Lazarus' longing to eat the crumbs that fell from the rich man's table must bring to mind the Syrophoenician woman. Once again, she is the model of faith and prayer. Both her prayer and the longing of Lazarus are met in the Holy Communion.

In ✠ Jesus' name. Amen.

FRIDAY OF REMINISCERE

Genesis 37:6-22
St. Matthew 21:33-46

In the name of the Father and of the ✠ Son and of the Holy Spirit. Amen.

Our world is run by the law. That is why children complain that life isn't fair. They know that it should be. They sense and complain about injustice.

Shepherds don't die for sheep; sheep die for shepherds. That is why shepherds raise them. Merchants do not deliberately drive themselves out of business by investing all their resources in one item that they will not sell. Vineyard owners don't pay for labor that wasn't performed, and they certainly don't send their sons to tenants after those tenants have already abused and killed servants.

These are the proverbs of men: "Fool me once, shame on you; fool me twice, shame on me;" "Don't throw good money after bad;" and "There is no such thing as a free lunch." But these are the proverbs of the Lord: "Free lunch;" "Good money after bad, after bad, after bad;" and "I'll keep loving you no matter how much you cheat on Me." Or as it says in the Holy Scripture, "Come to me, all who labor and are heavy laden, and I will give you rest" (Matt. 11:28) and "Go again, love a woman who is loved by another man and is an adulteress, even as the Lord loves the children of Israel, though they turn to other gods and love cakes of raisins" (Hos. 3:1).

We all like the idea of a second chance, but how many times must Hosea buy Gomer back out of prostitution? After three or four times, it certainly seems a bit much. How many times do you loan your alcoholic sister $10,000 when she has never paid you back in the past? How long can a woman endure the ongoing affair of an unfaithful husband? Why do we lock our doors at night? We can see a second or even a third, maybe a fourth chance, but after that we've reached our limit. Constant forgiveness in the face of abuse is nearly unimaginable and clearly reckless.

And that is the staggering shock of the grace of our Lord Jesus Christ. It is constant; even in the face of great and terrible, repeated, habitual sins, He does not stop. He loves us to the end. This great ongoing mercy and love does not come about because of us. The Christ loves us, to be sure, but His grace is not driven by His love for us. His grace is driven instead by His love for the Father. He obeys His Father's will. He fulfills His office, lays down His life, and takes it up again for His Father. And His Father loves Him for it.

The Son goes to the vineyard, knowing what they will do to Him, not simply because He loves those who kill Him, though He does, but He goes mainly because His Father sends Him.

He will take the kingdom from those rotten tenants and give it to others. He will give it to the Gentiles—that is the word there, not nation or people, but Gentiles—who produce the kingdom's fruits. What are those fruits? Brokenness. For He immediately says, "Whosoever shall fall on this stone shall be broken; but on whomsoever it shall fall, it will grind him to powder"(KJV). There is no way to get out of this unscathed. The fruit of the kingdom is to be broken: "The sacrifices of God are a broken spirit; a broken and contrite heart, O God, you will not despise" (Ps. 51:17).

Does this mean no Jew can inherit the kingdom? God forbid! Our Lord Himself is a Jew, as is His holy mother, and as are all the holy apostles. A Jew who is broken and gives up His Jewishness can enter the kingdom, not as a man, proud and full of honor, but as a child and a bride. So also, the Gentiles must give up their ethnicity. They must give up their identity among men and be broken. For the sacrifices of God are a broken spirit.

The stone the builders rejected falls upon us harshly, but in mercy. He breaks not only us, but He also breaks our chains. And He gives us a kingdom we do not deserve. We reap where we did not sow. We live in palaces we did not build. We have a husband who should not take us back or love us, but who does. What a mystery and a joy it is to be baptized into this kingdom of grace, not of the Law and justice, but of grace and mercy. God be praised! His goodness defies all reason and experience. This is most certainly marvelous in our eyes.

In ✛ *Jesus' name. Amen.*

Saturday of Reminiscere

Genesis 27:6-40
St. Luke 15:11-32

In the name of the Father and of the ✠ *Son and of the Holy Spirit. Amen.*

This parable stands before us as "the pearl of parables," "the gospel in the gospel" of our Lord Jesus Christ. It is the last of three parables. First comes the lost sheep; then the lost coin; and then this, the lost, or prodigal, son. These parables all illustrate that God seeks unworthy men to love and to save. They were spoken especially to the Pharisees because the Pharisees did not like the company that our Lord kept. St. Luke records, "And the Pharisees and the scribes grumbled, saying, 'This man receives sinners and eats with them'" (Luke 15:2). Our Lord responded to that complaint with these parables—ours the last, and most poignant, of the three. They are meant to explain why Jesus receives and eats with sinners and to shame the Pharisees for their failure to love their neighbors.†

The parable of the prodigal son, as it is commonly known, is, in fact, an allegorical history of man. It shows man in his innocence, in his rebellion, and, finally, in his redemption. It is an allegory of conversion, but it is also an allegory of the life of Christ because the life of Christ and the lives of His children are closely intermingled. The life Christ lived, He lived as the new Adam. The parable shows the ready character of divine grace. The Lord wants to take us back again. It is also a description of what is to be a Christian, to repent and return and to find that it was God who was working on you all along.

---

† Spence-Jones, H. D. M., ed. *The Pulpit Commentary: St. Luke* Vol. II (Bellingham, WA: Logos Research Systems, Inc., 2004), pp. 45-46. Spence-Jones provided the idea of the parable as history, poem, and prophecy and also inspired some of my language here.

The parable is also a kind of poem. Its refrain, "My son was dead, and is alive again, was lost, and is found," rings forever as the great song and joy of heaven. The angels rejoice over one sinner who repents, and they are nearly as happy, as giddy, as the Father Himself when a prodigal returns. Of course, it is we who were dead and are alive, who were lost and are found, who should be overcome with joy and laughter. But as in all things, our joy pales in comparison to those whose will is perfectly at one with the Father. We are the beneficiaries, but they appreciate it and are happier for it than we are. Such are the mysteries of heaven.

This parable is also prophetic. It speaks directly to us. It both reproves and encourages us, for we have been the prodigal son, and we have also been the elder brother. The parable is both Law and Gospel for the prodigal son. He should repent and stop being wasteful and stupid, but the father loves him with forgiveness and acceptance. It is also Law and Gospel for the elder brother. He is tempted to jealousy and judging, but he also is invited into the feast by the father's grace.

The parable receives a particularly bright light by being set alongside the account of Jacob's deception of Isaac. Grace comes to unfaithful sons and usurping liars, not to those who have a claim by birth or by works. For us Gentiles in particular, Jacob is our patron saint, the lesser, the second born, the usurper, the lying, unfaithful son who gets the blessing that belongs to another. We get the blessing that belongs to the faithful Son, Jesus. We are welcomed back to the feast despite our sins.

Whatever we have been—wasteful or judgmental, lying or arrogant—let us now again be repentant. He who is found, and found alive, is welcomed back into His Father's embrace in perfect, unexpected grace. We were lost. We are found. We were dead. We are now alive. The feast is before us. The Father has come out to entreat us, to beckon us to come and eat. Let us eat.

In ✠ Jesus' name. Amen.

The Third Sunday in Lent—Oculi

Jeremiah 26:1-15
Ephesians 5:1-9
St. Luke 11:14-28

In the name of the Father and of the ✠ Son and of the Holy Spirit. Amen.

Our Lord suffered many accusations before His crucifixion. It was said that He broke the Sabbath (Mark 3:1-6; John 5:16, 9:16); that He blasphemed (Mark 2:7, 14:64); that He was a deceiver (Matt. 27:63); that He claimed to be the king of the Jews (Mark 15:2); that He claimed to be the Messiah, the Son of God, and the Son of Man (Mark 14:61-62); that He misled the Jewish people and forbade payment of taxes to Caesar (Luke 23:2); and that He created a dangerous situation in which the Romans might intervene and abolish Jewish self-governance and even the temple (John 11:48).† But no charge was so blatantly evil as this: "He casts out demons by Beelzebul, the prince of demons."

The Lord's response to this is uncharacteristically logical. It reads almost like Aquinas. First off, He says, no kingdom divided against itself can stand. Satan is not against Satan. How then could Satan help anyone cast out demons? Secondly, if such a thing were possible, then it would be the only way to cast out demons. Either no one casts out demons by Beelzebul or everyone casting out demons does so by Beelzebul. Thus, if you don't take this back, your own sons will accuse you. Because if you insist on accusing Me of this, you are also accusing them. Finally, this ought to convince you of the lunacy of your accusation. The pagan Egyptian magicians could recognize the finger of God in the destructive miracles of Moses. Can you not see that I am casting

---

† This list of accusations and references is taken from John P. Meier, *A Marginal Jew, Rethinking the Historical Jesus: Volume Two, Mentor, Message, and Miracles* (New Haven; London: Yale University Press, 1994), p. 551.

out demons by the same finger of God, but for healing? The kingdom of God has arrived. I am King Messiah, and I am here for all who are mute, blind, and deaf. I am here for you. I do not bring you plagues and judgment. I bring you mercy and healing.

Then we get a little story and a warning. The story is the parable of the strong man. Satan is the strong man. He guards his palace. He has to guard it because he has stolen it, and he knows that it doesn't really belong to him. Along comes the stronger man, the Christ, God in the flesh of a man, who takes away the armor in which Satan trusted. The stronger man then takes the spoils for Himself.

We are the palace and the spoils. The Father says to the Son, "You are my Son; today I have begotten you. Ask of me, and I will make the [Gentiles] your heritage, and the ends of the earth your possession" (Ps. 2:7-8). The broken strong man has that in which he trusted taken away. What does the devil trust? He trusts the Law and justice. He remembers the Law in the garden before the fall: "You may surely eat of every tree of the garden, but of the tree of the knowledge of good and evil you shall not eat, for in the day that you eat of it you shall surely die" (Gen. 2:16-17). He was prepared to face the God of wrath, but not the man of mercy. The devil is not as strong as God become a man.

The Lord has taken away that in which the devil trusted. He has taken away the Law and justice and replaced them with mercy and sacrifice. The devil's strength, that by which he held us captive, was our sin. But the Lord forgives sins through the sacrifice of the Son. His greater strength is His love and His mercy. The devil's strength and armor are taken away. The demons are exiled and driven out, and mute men speak.

Then comes the warning. If a demon is cast out of the body but not out of the soul, it will come back with a vengeance. The Lord is not merely sparing the man from the demon's control over his mouth; He is freeing him from the control and accusations of the demons. No other exorcist can do this and, therefore, no other exorcist, even as no other physician, can really help or aid us. Jesus is the exorcist and physician that we desperately need.

This exorcism and healing is a historical account. It is not a parable. It really happened, but that doesn't mean that is all it is. The history of God's people and His interaction with them is never just stuff that happened for the sake of happening. The history of Israel, both large and small, is an allegory of the Christian. In this case, the mute man speaks. But mute men can't speak. If they do, they aren't mute.

I believe that I cannot believe. I confess that I cannot confess. I am mute. I am blind. I am lame. Yet the Holy Spirit has called me by the Gospel—and behold! Usurper, liar, demon cooperator that I am, I believe. I confess that Jesus is the Christ, the Son of the Living God, for it has been revealed to me by the Father in heaven in His holy Word. I speak. I see. I run. I have been bought back, redeemed, and my accuser stands silent. He tempts me, to be sure. He seeks to deceive and mislead me. But he is now mute. He has lost his sting and threat. He has no sins to point out. For I am baptized and forgiven, and I commune with the Holy Trinity, as the very bride of Christ, in His risen body and blood.

The Lord has plucked my feet out of the net and sent him who hunted my soul away without weapons or a way back. I am saved, and my eyes are ever toward the Lord.

In ✠ Jesus' name. Amen.

Monday of Oculi

2 Kings 5:1-15a
St. Luke 4:23-30

In the name of the Father and of the ✠ Son and of the Holy Spirit. Amen.

The context for today's Gospel is our Lord's first sermon in Nazareth. He had been baptized and tempted. Full of the Spirit, He had begun His ministry in Galilee. When He goes to the synagogue in Nazareth, He reads from Isaiah 61. Then, as St. Luke writes:

> [H]e rolled up the scroll and gave it back to the attendant and sat down. And the eyes of all in the synagogue were fixed on him. And he began to say to them, "Today this Scripture has been fulfilled in your hearing." And all spoke well of him and marveled at the gracious words that were coming from his mouth. And they said, "Is not this Joseph's Son?" (Luke 4:20-22)

They "spoke well of Him." Sort of. They aren't completely innocent when they ask, "Is not this Joseph's son?" They know the claims, the stories of angels, and the like. And that is probably what prompts Him to bring up the bit about physicians healing themselves and the history of hard-hearted rejection in Israel.

They prove His prophecy of prophets being rejected in their hometowns with their next breath. They are no longer speaking well of Him; they are filled with rage and ready to kill Him.

Satan tempted our Lord to throw Himself down from the temple. That failed, so he fills a crowd with rage that they might throw Him down the cliff. But the Lord has come to the earth not to be cast down, but to be lifted up. He will be killed, but it will be as a sacrifice, outside the City of Peace, not in Nazareth. And He won't be rescued by angels either. He will be forsaken by His Father. He won't heal Himself, but He will be wounded for our transgressions, crushed for our iniquities, striped by the lash for our healing.

Here is what He read in the synagogue, what was fulfilled in their hearing:

> "The Spirit of the Lord is upon me, because he has anointed me to proclaim good news to the poor. He has sent me to proclaim liberty to the captives and recovering of sight to the blind, to set at liberty those who are oppressed, to proclaim the year of the Lord's favor." (Luke 4:18-19)

This He does in perfect love. He submits to their hate. He lets them do their worst. He embraces the poverty of the poor as the captives drag Him into their captivity and the blind gouge out His eyes. He gives us His liberty for our oppression. He gives us life for murdering Him. All this He does to proclaim the good news, the year of the Lord's favor, the jubilee of forgiveness, and thus the end of slavery to sin and death.

For this He has been anointed and filled with the Spirit. This He has fulfilled that we might dare to call Him Lord, to be His people by grace. Never were a people more undeserving than we, but that is the character of grace. It is bestowed upon those who are unworthy. By grace, we are the heirs of the widow in Zarephath, of Naaman from Syria, the children of Abraham raised up from stones.

In ✚ Jesus' name. Amen.

TUESDAY OF OCULI

2 Kings 4:1-7
St. Matthew 18:15-22

In the name of the Father and of the ✠ Son and of the Holy Spirit. Amen.

At first read, Matthew 18's instructions about how to handle a sinning brother seem like straight-up ethics. The Law given by the Holy Spirit to Moses had already instructed us on this. It states, "You shall not hate your brother in your heart, but you shall reason frankly with your neighbor, lest you incur sin because of him" (Lev. 19:17).

The law given here in Matthew 18 perfectly conforms to the rabbinic reading of Leviticus. If someone sins against you, warn him and try to win him back. If he will not listen to the Word of God, which is the most reasonable thing in the universe, then he is to be to you as a heathen. Telling it to the Church is not a step meant to bring more pressure upon the unrepentant, but it is to vindicate the one who brought the first two warnings. Its purpose is to show the Church that the offended party did not refuse to forgive; instead, when he sought reconciliation, he was rebuked and refused.

But we miss the point if we miss the context. And we usually do. Why? Because we are just like the fallen rabbis; we like rules and lists and steps. Repent.

Our Lord upheld all of the Law, not just this. This is neither His most important law nor His favorite. He also preaches against lust and anger and a number of other things. But those things are never His main point. Never. This particular bit of legalese comes smack-dab in the middle of a parable about lost sheep. The point is that the angels rejoice over a single sinner who repents. St. Peter's question about how often to forgive and the parable of the unmerciful servant, who was forgiven an enormous debt and then refused to forgive, are about lavish forgiveness for the repentant. The rabbis weren't so generous. They advocated that a man should be rebuked and forgiven three times. After that, if he committed the same sin, he was not to be rebuked anymore but let go in his sins.

We aren't so generous either. But we tend to err in the other way. We use Matthew 18 like Miranda rights. If one Christian fails to follow the process perfectly, the whole case is thrown out. Kyrie Eleison! As though the pot can't call the kettle black, or as though the pot's blackness somehow excused the blackness of the kettle. The point, for our Lord, is not that we should look the other way, but that both pot and kettle need repentance and grace.

St. Peter indicates that he is onto the way of the Lord. The kingdom is built on grace, on mercy, on forgiveness. The Lord is into repentance, forgiveness, cleansing, new starts. So St. Peter suggests more than double the generosity of the rabbis—not three, but seven. Bright as St. Peter was, the Lord demonstrates how beyond all of us His grace and mercy are. Not seven times, but seven times seventy, which is not to say four hundred ninety, but forever. He forgives as many sins as you've got. He even forgives more sins than you've done, more than you need. The Lord doesn't give up on you.

His grace is extreme—radical and even crazy, if judged in the ways of men. But this is what makes it grace. That is its character. It is not for those who deserve it even a little bit or for those who try hard and are sincere. It is not for those who properly follow all of the steps and rules. It is for those who are unworthy. The Lord doesn't speak the Law for the sake of those who are looking for steps to take and rules to keep. He speaks the Law for those who are dead in their trespasses and don't know it. He preaches the Law to warn us and kill us, that we would throw ourselves upon His mercy.

And how much will His mercy cover? How many times will He forgive? As much as you need and more. For His mercy endures forever.

In ✠ Jesus' name. Amen.

Wednesday of Oculi

Exodus 20:12-24
St. Matthew 15:1-20

In the name of the Father and of the ✠ Son and of the Holy Spirit. Amen.

What comes out of the mouth proceeds from the heart. This defiles a person. For out of the heart come evil thoughts, murder, adultery, sexual immorality, theft, false witness, and slander. These are what defile a person.

Evil thoughts, murder, adultery, sexual immorality, theft, false witness, and slander do not come from our limbs or from our members, but from our hearts. Our hearts are who we are. When we sin, we do not do something alien or out of character, but we do that which is truly of ourselves. When we sin, we expose ourselves, our hearts, our true person. For we are not basically good and decent people deep down. Deep down we are vile. We defile ourselves by what we say and what we do.

Lack of ceremonies does not defile a man, but neither is a lack of ceremonies a virtue. In fact, it is practically impossible to imagine piety without ceremony. Those whose hearts have been purified by the blood of Christ will confess His name, and they will respond to the confession with their bodies even as mothers hug their babies. It comes naturally. Pious, forgiven people will know and feel joy. Thus, they will treat holy things as holy—not to earn favor with God, but simply because they are thankful. But even if they didn't engage in any ceremony at all, that lack would not defile them.

The ceremony that the disciples were accused of neglecting—not washing their hands before eating—was not a moral imperative. It was only a ceremony. Condemning them for this lack of ceremony would be like us condemning someone for not making the sign of the cross or for not making it correctly or in the right place.

The Pharisees were so far from the kingdom that they thought their ceremonies trumped God's Law. There was a beauty in their system, to be sure. No doubt, it had been born in piety, but it became corrupt, and they caved in to their baser desires. They forgot the point: Hand washing was supposed to remind them of the need to be cleansed by God, to receive forgiveness, and to remind them that their food and sustenance came from God. They became superstitious, replacing the creation for the Creator, and replacing faith with ceremonies.

Let us not judge them too harshly, though, because this is a warning for us. The antichrist sits in the temple of God. The wolf dons sheep's clothing. Externals can be faked, and abuse comes quickly to the evil hearts of men. In fact, there is no moral injunction to pray before every meal. We do it in freedom for all the same reasons that the Pharisees engaged in hand washing, but it is hard not to judge our brothers and sisters in Christ who don't pray before eating. We do sort of think that it is required of Christians or that God expects it. Repent.

After this exhortation from our Lord comes the Syrophoenician woman we heard from a couple of weeks ago. She has ceremonies also. She forms her prayer in a formal way. She falls down on her face at our Lord's feet. She recites the Kyrie, or, perhaps, she invents the Kyrie. But she is different from the Pharisees. She is humble in her desperation, willing to be a dog, and she is bold in her confidence that God is good and will deliver her and her daughter from demons.

St. Matthew's point is clear: What comes out of her, "Kyrie Eleison," purifies her and shows her heart. Let it be the same in and out of us. Let the Kyrie come out of our hearts and purify us, for we are also desperate. We need grace. We need mercy. We need Christ. Thanks be to God, we have Him, crucified and risen, in the Holy Communion. There is something that can go in that can purify and cleanse us.

In ✠ Jesus' name. Amen.

Thursday of Oculi

Jeremiah 7:1-7
St. Luke 4:38-44

In the name of the Father and of the ✠ Son and of the Holy Spirit. Amen.

The mother-in-law of St. Peter was suffering from a terrible fever. She is a type of our nature. We are struck with a terrible fever; we burn with unlawful lusts for diverse objects, for perversions of the flesh, and also for fame, money, and recognition. We lust for that which the Lord has not given. Repent.

The fever of passion that threatens to consume us is not lesser than bodily fever or sickness. Indeed, sin is worse. Its cause is easier to diagnose, perhaps, but its scars and damage are also far more severe and its treatment more difficult. Avarice and lust, luxury and ambition, anger and pride: These are our fevers, though to our shame, we've often counted them as friends. Repent.

And in your repentance, notice how long-suffering the Lord is. His displeasure over the malicious self-righteousness of the Pharisees, the greed of the tax collectors, the worldliness of the Sanhedrin, and the foolishness of the Greeks—all of which caused pain and suffering for His people and the world—did not cause Him to desert them or us.

Yes, He was vexed by their guilt and complicity. He was shocked at their brazenness and impenitence. He was outraged by their blasphemy. But He remembered His mercy. He sought to soften their hard and unbelieving hearts. Sometimes He did this by teaching, sometimes by freeing them from sin and demons, sometimes by examples, and sometimes by healing. But always He served in mercy, to show them the heart of His Father, to proclaim His name, to reconcile and redeem.

Always, whatever He did was leading to the end of sin and all its consequences, was leading to His sacrifice on the cross. He healed St. Peter's mother-in-law not simply because He felt sorry for her, though He did. Mainly, He healed her because He was doing away with the cause of all sickness and death, because He had come for her salvation, because He loved and wanted her to be in His kingdom.

We know He is the Christ. So too did the demons, but the demons were missing an essential component. They left off "suffering." Our Lord is the suffering Christ, the One who lays down His life as a ransom. We are not demons. We have faith. Let us speak, confess, praise, thank, and give witness to this joy and truth. Let us proclaim again His death in the eating of His body and the drinking of His blood. Let us pray that He remove the fevers from us according to His promise, for by grace we are His people. Nay, more: We are His bride.

In ✚ Jesus' name. Amen.

FRIDAY OF OCULI

Numbers 20:2-3, 6-13
St. John 4:5-42

In the name of the Father and of the ✠ Son and of the Holy Spirit. Amen.

The disciples return to find our Lord talking to the equivalent of "the town tart." Their sense of embarrassment is almost palpable. To their credit, they restrain themselves from asking about the incident as the woman departs.

She leaves behind a water jar, reminding us how the jars for hand washing in Cana were forever ruined for that purpose when they were filled with wine. She has abandoned the old dependencies and idolatries. She leaves the jar behind. She is now free from her need to be cleansed and therefore also her fear of meeting her neighbors. Indeed, she publishes abroad the open invitation to come and see, adding that this may be the Christ.

This is a bit of a surprise for she had begun in a surly enough way, treating Jesus as a precocious stranger. But then something changed. She gave Him the respect due a rabbi, calling Him "Lord," or *Kyrie*, though this is often translated as "Sir." It is surprising to us because He had been quite harsh with her, though not as harsh as He would be. We think this would turn her off, but instead it catches her attention. It even gains Him some respect. In this, at least, she seems to recognize that whatever or whoever it is that is speaking, He is no vain flatterer and He has nothing to sell.

She had tried to treat Him as though He were ordinary, but then she discovered that He is not. It seems much the same with both Pilate and Herod. Was there something of our Lord's holiness that was communicated in body language and manner, despite His ugliness and sorrow? I don't know. But I do know that we are always sending messages, communicating with posture, the tilt of our heads, the line of our mouths, and so forth. How differently does a man without sin, without self-love and self-worship, appear in the eyes of fallen men? The Pharisees tried to ignore that aspect of our Lord. I think they were pretending because it was apparently evident to Gentiles who had nothing to lose by admitting it. But that is simply another indication of the hard hearts of the Pharisees.

The Lord made one of His few crystal-clear prophecies to this woman. She said, "I know that Messiah is coming." And He said, "I AM, the One who is speaking." The KJV again inserts "He" after "I AM." I find that distracting from the claim that He is making. He is the Messiah, to be sure, which is what "I AM He" would mean, but the point here is that the Messiah is the God of Abraham in the flesh who is worshiped in spirit and truth. He claims the divine name. Thus does this encounter end with the woman proclaiming Him to her neighbors and saying, "Is not He the Christ?" Her invitation works; they come.

Notice, too, the distinction between this Samaritan invitation, that the Lord stay with them, in contrast to the crowds who sought to take Him by force and make Him a slave-king who would make bread for them or the crowd in Nazareth who tried to throw Him off the cliff. These Samaritans have faith. And get this: Our Lord stays. In the language of the KJV, He abode there two days.

By His grace they confess that He is the Christ, the Savior of the world. Don't forget that this woman was the town tart. Was. Not any more. The village is a city of Samaria. These are not the chosen people. The kingdom is for outsiders—tarts and Samaritans, tax collectors and mercenaries, fisherman and shepherds—made into the children of Abraham.

We live in dark days. Our own sins, like the Samaritan woman's, also threaten to overcome us. But God is good. The Messiah comes in His risen body and blood. He bestows living water. He forgives sins and welcomes Gentiles. He is the Christ, our Christ, the Savior of the world.†

In ✠ Jesus' name. Amen.

† Part of these ideas come from Phillip McFadyen, *Open Door on John: A Gospel for Our Time* (London: Triangle, 1998), pp. 24-25.

Saturday of Oculi

Daniel 13:1-62
St. John 8:1-11

In the name of the Father and of the ✠ Son and of the Holy Spirit. Amen.

St. Augustine, in his tractate on the woman caught in adultery,[†] notes the Messianic character of Psalm 45:3-4 as it relates to the account of this woman: "Gird your sword on your thigh, O mighty one, in your splendor and majesty! In Your majesty ride out victoriously for the cause of truth and meekness and righteousness; let your right hand teach you awesome deeds!"

As a teacher, Jesus brought truth; as a deliverer, He brought meekness; as a protector, He brought righteousness. His rule was based in these three things and not in the strength of violence. He had girded His sword to His thigh.

His truth made Him unassailable in argument. His meekness made Him popular with the masses. So His enemies laid a stumbling block for His righteousness. "Here," they thought, "is a weakness."

The Law had commanded that adulterers be stoned. Surely the Law could not command what was unjust. If any man should naysay the Law, he would be detected as unjust, that is, unrighteous.

Therefore they laid the trap. They sought to play one gift against another. They said among themselves, "If He approves the stoning of a woman caught in adultery, He will appear as though He is not gentle or meek and lose His popularity. If He urges that she be let go, He will act contrary to the Law and be unrighteous. Doubtless, that is what He

---

† Schaff, Philip, ed. *Nicene and Post-Nicene Fathers,* First Series, vol. 7. (Peabody, MA: Hendrickson Publishers, Inc, 1995), p. 198.

will do. He will demand she be let go. Then we will accuse Him of being an enemy of the Law, against Moses, and being also deserving of death."

But fallen men who prepare such snares always stick their own necks in first. Behold! The Lord keeps His righteousness and upholds the holy Law without departing from His meekness and gentleness. He for whom the snare was laid was not taken, but rather they were taken who laid it because they believed not on Him who could pull them out of the net. Your mother wasn't far off when she taught you not to point because four fingers always point back at you.

They made this terrible strategic error because they themselves were enemies of the Law. You have heard, O Jews! You have heard, O Pharisees! You have heard, O teachers of the Law! But you have not understood: Jesus Christ is Himself the Law-giver and the Law-fulfiller. He writes with His finger on the ground as the finger of God once wrote the Law in stone. But He is come in mercy. His sword is now girded to His thigh. He writes not on barren stone, but in living earth. The finger of God now replants the garden. He writes not that which condemns, but He writes a promise.

You have heard, "Let the Law be fulfilled. Let the adulterers be stoned," but is it by punishing sinners that the Law is fulfilled? No. That is only consequence, not fulfillment. The execution of adulterers does not recast the marriage bed any more than the execution of murderers might bring back the dead. The Law is a harsh mistress. She demands perfect obedience, and she punishes those who fail. We all fail, but false accusations are as bad as that which they falsely accused, and even righteous accusations are dangerous for those whose lives are not perfect. We all fail. The Law demands and punishes. She does not fulfill.

Let each then consider himself. How do you stand against the Law? How will you fare when judged according to its just, yet strict, demands? Confess, O man: "I am a sinner. I cannot cast stones. I cannot fulfill the Law's demands."

If the Lord had said, "Let the adulteress go," He would have proved Himself unjust. The Law is holy. But if He had said, "Go ahead and stone her," He would have been party to an unjust lynching. For there was no one righteous enough to judge her, save Him. So He said, "Whosoever is without sin, let him cast the first stone."

This is the voice of justice: "Let her, the sinner, be punished, yes—but not by sinners. Let the Law be fulfilled, but not by the transgressors of the Law." When they have been driven off by the Law, the Lord exercises His divine prerogative. Let not your eye be evil because He is good. He can be generous with His goods as He sees fit. He is without sin. He could have cast the stones and fulfilled the Law. But remember, O Christian—remember and never forget—He has girded His sword to His thigh. He comes in meekness and peace. Isn't that the point of the angels to the shepherds in their fields? The Lord has come to earth with His sword girded to His thigh. The Lord comes in peace.

There is another way to fulfill the Law, to end the war: He who is without sin can take the stones for her. He can make Himself the holy substitute. He—the Law-giver of Moses—can fulfill the Law in Himself, both by obeying it and also by allowing it to do to Him everything it should have done to her and to us. He is pure and He is just and He is a worthy sacrifice, more than enough to pay for all the sins of the world, more than enough to pay for her sins and for yours. He is clean, without sin, and therefore pure enough to make the judgment and to bear the consequences.

He has girded His sword to His thigh. What a joyous truth this is. He rode into the death trap, the vineyard where the workers had killed His Father's servants, into the midst of the angry mob, and He put the scarlet letter upon Himself. "Here am I, kill Me." He says, "I am the sinner for sinners, the scapegoat, the substitute, the whole burnt offering, the ransom, and the mercy seat." He rode with truth, with meekness, and with righteousness. "Neither do I accuse you," He said.

No sweeter words have ever been spoken in all of history. The sword is girded to His thigh.

In ✠ Jesus' name. Amen.

The Fourth Sunday in Lent—Laetare

Exodus 16:2-21
Galatians 4:21-31
St. John 6:1-15

In the name of the Father and of the ✠ Son and of the Holy Spirit. Amen.

The boy has five loaves of bread and two fish. That is not an insignificant amount. It is a grocery sack full of food. Think of how many peanut butter sandwiches you can make with five loaves of bread. It was certainly more than enough for him and his family. Still, what is that among so many? He might have enough food for thirty or forty people if they all eat just a little, but there are five thousand men plus women and children.

Of course it is a child, not an adult, who shows up with the food. The Lord is into children. And of course the food is not pomegranates or figs or mutton or beef, but bread and fish. The Lord is into bread and fish. It could have been shelter or clothing, which they needed, but it wasn't. It was food, because the Lord is into feeding.

But how does Andrew know the exact contents of the boy's grocery sack? Has he been out looking for food already, taking a survey, making a list? And what do they do with the leftovers? Does the boy get them, at least five loaves' worth? I don't know.

Some liberal scholars have read this as a miracle of sharing. It is not that our Lord multiplied the bread and fish, but rather that the people saw the boy's generosity and were so moved by it that they all started pulling out the food they had hidden away and kept for themselves. The miracle is that they learned to share. But if that were the case—and this is no miracle at all even though it is called a sign by St. John—then why are they given as much bread and fish as they want? That is not the way to share. If the message here is that we should all share resources and stop hoarding, so that no one is rich and no one is poor, then it would be a fable meant to teach constraint and moderation, maybe even self-sacrifice. But this is described as a feast. Each has as much as he wants, and there are leftovers remaining that can barely be contained. Sharing doesn't make a feast.

The liberals are, however, on to something. The Lord does use bread from creation, from a boy, to feed all the people there, even the evil people. He does not provide there in the same fashion that He provided for the Israelites in the desert. In this case, He does not create from nothing, but He multiplies what is there. It is sort of a cross between the widow's oil with Elijah and the manna in the desert with Moses, both of whom show up at the transfiguration. That is no mere coincidence.

St. John reports that when Jesus asked Philip what to do, that He Himself knew what He would do. That certainly means that the Lord was not in doubt about the fate of these people. He knew He would provide. I am not so sure that it has to mean that He knew about the boy's bread and fish. I suspect that He proceeds as a reaction to what the disciples say and do. Andrew has found some bread but is in despair. "What is it among so many?" he asks. So the Lord shows Him what it is among so many. By grace, it is plenty, more than enough, a feast with leftovers.

Here is the point: The boy is a historical figure, but he is also an allegory of the Christian. The Christian brings his offerings to God, and God does great things with them. The apostles are also historic, but they are, at the same time, an allegory or type of pastors. The Lord is not exactly teaching us to share, but He is showing us that we have a part in His kingdom, that He includes us, that He blesses and uses the works of our hands, that our good works are in fact good, and that by them He provides for the world, for church and for neighbor. He knows what He is going to do. He is going to feed the people. What the disciples say and do, or what the people give or hold, will determine how He feeds the people. If the boy had had a flask of wine with him, there probably would have been wine at this feast, and plenty for everyone.

If there is a stewardship lesson here, it is not that if we do not share and cooperate we will starve. Neither is it that the Lord will multiply back unto us whatever we give, so that if you give a dollar you will get ten back or at least get ten dollars' worth of blessing. As far as we know, the boy went home without any leftovers. He gave away his bread and fish, and though he got enough to eat, he got nothing else. It didn't make him rich. If there is a stewardship lesson here, it is that the dollar you give in faith, out of love for neighbor, will do more good given than it will in your pocket, and that what you do for and in the kingdom, God will multiply and bless.

But more significantly, in terms of stewardship, the reality is that the Lord gives you a choice and freedom in these things. The crowd isn't lectured about sharing or preparing. No wild promises are made about how their lives will go if they only behave better and give more. The boy simply moves out of love, in freedom, because he wants to, and the Lord blesses it, multiplies it, and provides for thousands. The boy, though unnamed and mainly without honor for his gift in this life, played a most significant part, more significant than the apostles, to be sure.

Your part in God's kingdom is also significant. Your service to neighbor, family, state, and church is seen and blessed by God. He multiplies your prayers, efforts, and gifts in order to provide for His children.

But neither is that the main thing here. This miracle, like all the miracles, is eucharistic. We pray for daily bread not to remind God that we need it, but that He would lead us to realize that He is the giver and that we would receive it with thanksgiving. That word "thanksgiving" happens to be the English translation of the Greek word "eucharist." Apart from the death and resurrection of Jesus Christ, there would be no mercy and no providence, no bread for hungry people. It is only because the Father has reconciled us to Himself in the Son and declared us righteous that He loves us and that anyone, believer or not, has anything close to what is necessary for this body and life. The Lord never just gives bread, the bare necessities and nothing more. That is why bread brings pleasure and is subject to abuse. Bread is not simply vitamins and nutrients; it is food. So also do flowers and the landscape display beauty. They are not just practical. Words bring not only knowledge, but also laughter. This is the character of our Lord. He is generous. He is merciful. He is loving.

Food is more than simple practicality or base necessity. Food is fellowship and pleasure. The Lord doesn't only provide on the mountain for the hungry and unworthy. He also provides for Himself. He joins them. He who did not eat when the devil tempted Him with bread in the desert now eats bread in the desert with sinners. Again: He who did not eat when the devil tempted Him with bread in the desert now eats bread in the desert made lush and full of green grass, with sinners made saints.

If there is some stewardship stuff, some vocational examples, mixed into all this, it should come as no surprise. This is simply who God's people are: They are His stewards and officers in this world. When the Scriptures speak of them, they are described as such. But the real thing here is that the Lord loves, welcomes, feeds, and eats with sinners. And as He did then, so He does now, and so He will do forever. The Lord welcomes, feeds, and eats with sinners.

It doesn't matter so much how the bread and wine got here today for our communion, who paid for it, who prepared it, and so forth. It doesn't matter much, but it does matter some. Some of you gathered here today are responsible for it; you did it. You gave the money that paid for it. You went and picked it up. You counted out the bread and measured the wine and set out the sacred vessels. Others just showed up—like people who followed Jesus on a three-day journey into the desert. That is not just okay; that is blessed by the Lord. For what matters is that the Lord provides. He knows what He will do. He has gathered you for Himself. He will feed you with His body and blood and thereby bestow His forgiveness and blessing upon you.

Thus do we have joy and even a feast in the midst of the fast, as sinners cleansed, loved, and fed in a desert made lush with grass.

In ✠ Jesus' name. Amen.

Monday of Laetare

1 Kings 3:16-28
St. John 2:13-25

In the name of the Father and of the ✠ Son and of the Holy Spirit. Amen.

The money changers and livestock sellers were providing a necessary service. It is not sinful to sell that which is honorable, even good. It is not even wrong to profit from the venture of supplying the Church with the goods she needs.

The problem, of course, was where they were doing it. They were doing business in the court of the Gentiles and thereby denying the Gentiles a place for prayer; it was a refusal of Isaiah's proclamation that the temple is a house of prayer for all people. The second part of the problem is that they were seeking to buy and sell in the place of God's self-giving.

St. Augustine sees a type. The merchants who sell sheep are selling the souls of the faithful for a profit, misleading them with earthly concerns in the holy place, distracting them from the things of God. To sell God's people is to sell sheep. Next, he sees the sellers of doves as those who purport to sell the Holy Ghost, to deceive the people into thinking they can buy forgiveness. And finally, those who sell oxen are those who try to sell the prophets and the apostles. For St. Paul says of the apostolic ministers, "Do not muzzle the ox." Thus, the last group is the most diabolical because they would mislead us by abuse of the Holy Scriptures and cover up our sin with sin.

We tend to hear such allegorizing too literally. All Augustine means is that the spirit of the money changers is present still in the Church today and is still a danger. What our Lord did was illustrative of what He still does and what must be done. In no way does Augustine mean these things weren't actually happening as described. Nor is it really fair to see Augustine looking for some deeper spiritual meaning. He simply recognizes the reality that the devil continues to attack the Lord's children in the same ways. We should note his tactics and strategies and realize that what happened then is still happening now. In fact, for Augustine and all the fathers, everything that is recorded in the Scriptures is applicable to our lives. So then we should also examine ourselves and consider how we have been party to and promoters of selling the sheep, the Holy Spirit, and the Scriptures. Then, of course, we should repent.

In any case, the making of the scourge is surely more symbolic than actually punitive. The Lord drives them off by moral force rather than physical abuse. They know they are wrong. They know they have defiled God's house. The Lord acts as every prophet would, but then every prophet was a type of the Messiah sent to proclaim God's Word to the people, to call them back to repentance and faith, to show them what God's mercy is and where God's mercy abides. The temple is the place of God's gracious presence, where the Holy Spirit is not bought or sold but instead comes by grace and promise. It is where God gives Himself away and where the people can be cleansed in order to pray and to praise God.

They know the Lord has spoken rightly with Isaiah's words. They do not doubt His justice. They make no excuse for their sin. But they do ask for a sign of His authority.

Here is the real point of this whole scene: His authority comes from being killed and raised. He is the temple. He is the sacrifice. He—who stands with scourge in hand—has the right to give away the Holy Spirit because He is scourged and killed as the sacrifice of mercy that the temple shows and delivers to all people. He is raised again that all people might have safe access to the Father through Him. That is the zeal that consumes Him and saves us.

In ✛ Jesus' name. Amen.

Tuesday of Laetare

Exodus 32:7-14
St. John 7:14-31

In the name of the Father and of the ✠ *Son and of the Holy Spirit. Amen.*

The entire purpose of the Sabbath was to give rest and re-creation, that is, wholeness. It is the only commandment that is a commandment to do nothing. Here is how to rightly worship the God of Abraham, Isaac, and Jacob: Do nothing.

It is a perverse marvel of our fallen flesh that we have such an incredible propensity for sin that, guided by the father of lies, we can turn "do nothing" into a work that must be performed.

In any case, the gift of circumcision predates the Sabbath regulations of Moses. Even more than that, the obvious theological principle, discerned by the faithful rabbis even before the Christ, was that danger of life nullified all Sabbath regulations. When the Lord said, "The Sabbath was made for man, not man for the Sabbath," He said nothing new.

But some of the rabbis and priests had been misled and deceived, and some were flat-out evil. Few of them had the theological discernment of their fathers. If they had, then they would not have questioned the obvious goodness of making whole on the Sabbath. Either that, or they were incapable of seeing that healing and the Sabbath were complementary and that one could not violate the other.

Sin makes us stupid. It makes it hard for us to make good choices in any part of our lives, and it makes it impossible for us to understand God's holy Word—not that God's Word is not clear. God's Word is clear. But we don't want to understand it when we are in our sin.

The rabbi's stupidity here in John 7 serves, however, to show that our Lord's wisdom is apart from the rabbis. It does not come from human sources or traditions. The Lord is the source and foundation in Himself. Their stupidity also serves as a warning for us. It is possible to have the trappings of orthodoxy and the correct formulations but to turn them on their heads, to turn "do nothing" into something we must do. Kyrie Eleison.

The rabbis at the time of our Lord's incarnation had knowledge without love. They did not discern the gracious character of the temple and the sacrifices. They did not understand that the Lord provides rest and re-creation for His people. Thus, their knowledge of the Law was evil. Without this understanding and faith, there is nothing. Without the gracious character of the temple and the sacrifices, etc., the God of Abraham is no different than the god of Mohammed. Kyrie Eleison! We are too weak for that. This, however, sadly, was the case for those lying rabbis. How else could they plot murder? The Law was not holy to them. It was an instrument for their own power and glory. Kyrie Eleison! God save us from this, the worst perversion that has ever been practiced on earth: turning the gracious Word of God into a weapon to oppress sinners.

The Lord does come in mercy, in *eleison*, despite us. He comes not for His own glory, but for His Father's glory. His Father's glory is to snatch us back from the devil. He comes not with His own words and understanding, but as the Holy Trinity's apostle to earth, to proclaim the year of jubilee without end, peace between God and men, the forgiveness of sins, the end of debts and slavery.

They did not seize Him, despite their plots, until He was ready. He was not only the victim; He was also the priest. When it was His hour—then, and not before—He laid down His life of His own accord, as a gracious, life-giving sacrifice. He brought to fulfillment the Sabbath, the laws of Moses, and the covenant with Abraham. By God's grace, many believed Him. And by God's grace—thanks be to God!—so do we. In the end, it wasn't His miracles or even His healing on the Sabbath that convinced them to believe in Him; it was the Holy Spirit. He convinced them to believe in the Son through the Son's preaching. That preaching opened the heart of the Father—whose desire was always to have them back—to the people, and they believed.

Here was ever the purpose of the Sabbath: to give rest and re-creation, to make whole. Here in the Sabbath gift is the constant character of God, whose mercy endures forever, and of His Christ, who has died to give men rest.

In ✠ Jesus' name. Amen.

Wednesday of Laetare

Ezekiel 36:23-28
St. John 9:1-38

In the name of the Father and of the ✠ Son and of the Holy Spirit. Amen.

At first, the man born blind knew only that our Lord was a prophet. The Pharisees claimed to know that Jesus was a sinner and sought to coerce the healed man into saying the same. His parents were little help; they were afraid of the Pharisees. I think this failure of the parents here is a bit of an allegory. The whole Jewish system was falling apart, and it is the Lord God Himself who is our true Father.

The Pharisees imply that even if Jesus had meant well in this healing, He had broken God's Law by healing on the Sabbath and therefore couldn't be trusted. Seven times the Gospels record Jesus' healing on the Sabbath. He was openly defiant of the Sanhedrin and the Pharisaic code. The parents of the man born blind were afraid, but He was not. He heals on the Sabbath because He has compassion. He is not glorifying Himself, nor is He seeking anyone's approval other than His Father's. He is sent by the Father to glorify Him. The Father is glorified when men are recaptured from the enemy and belong to Him once again, no matter what day of the week it is.

The man born blind refuses to implicate our Lord. He knows that he has felt the finger of God, that God has healed him, that this was not an evil thing. He will not throw his benefactor under the bus.

Though it is not the intended result, the evil of the Sanhedrin forces out of the man not an accusation, but a great confession. Though they do not intend it, their questioning pushes the man to consider our Lord in Messianic terms. What they meant for evil, God used for good.

They bring up the whole idea: From whence could this prophet have possibly come? His miracles are not only indisputable, but they bear the peculiar Messianic character foretold in Isaiah. As the man tells us, there are no healings of the blind in the Old Testament, not even one. Yet it is foretold that the Messiah will give the blind sight. This man, therefore, must be from God; more than that, He must be the Messiah Himself, the promised One who brings rest, light, healing, and joy.

Thank you, Sanhedrin, you have shined light by your evil and asked the critical question: From whence cometh this man?

Here is what is obvious to anyone paying attention: Either Jesus is the Messiah and the Pharisees have made the Law of God void and are actually in collusion with the demons, or the miracles performed by Jesus will turn out to be magic or falsehood with demons and the Pharisees are actually good. It is one or the other, but not both. It simply can't be that both Jesus and the Pharisees are good. Either Jesus is in the league with demons, or the Pharisees are, or they both are, but someone has to be.

But no demon ever healed a man of blindness. And no demon-possessed man, or those in collusion with demons, could ever appear without any flaw or sin. Ask our politicians and celebrities how fun it is to be examined up close. They suffer the scrutiny of the press. They always get caught in their imperfections. The sins of the Pharisees are obvious in their questioning. We don't even need to know any more to see that they are sinners. Jesus undergoes far more scrutiny than they do, and yet everyone, even Mohammed, knows that Jesus is good.

The Pharisees say that they know He is a sinner. We know that they are liars. They have no evidence. They cannot find any flaw in His teaching or in His behavior. They claim to be Moses' disciples but quote not one passage from Moses.

Imagine a teacher, not simply in whom no flaw or weakness was immediately evident, but in whom no flaw could be found even upon searching. It must have been amazing. The Pharisees are liars. Jesus speaks the truth. They are guilty, scheming men who seek their own glory. He is innocent and is moved by compassion.

The best they can do at the end is to simply accuse the blind man of having been born in his sins and throw him out. In effect, they deny the reality of the miracle before them.

Yet all of this serves our Lord's purpose. The Lord's work is shown in this man, for Jesus is the light in the world. He enlightens the eyes and hearts of men. Having seen the cruel perversion of God's Law in the Pharisees and the contrasting goodness of the Lord incarnate, the man born blind is ready to confess fully that Jesus is the Christ and thus to worship Him. Those whom the Pharisees cast out find a place at the Lord's table.

The lessons in this for us are too many to elaborate here. Suffice it for now to say that we aren't the man born blind; we are the Pharisees. We are not innocent or good. Left to ourselves, we would be damned in our sins. But the Lord comes in mercy for sinners, to seek and to save the lost. There is room at His table even for Pharisees, for He is the Christ and He forgives sins.

In ✠ *Jesus' name. Amen.*

Thursday of Laetare

2 Kings 4:25-38
St. Luke 7:11-16

In the name of the Father and of the ✠ Son and of the Holy Spirit. Amen.

There are only three resurrections recorded in the Gospels. Only John has Lazarus. Only Luke has the widow's son in Nain. The third is the raising of Jairus' daughter in Capernaum, recorded by both Mark and Luke. If you were keeping score, you might have noticed that Matthew doesn't have any.

St. Augustine says these are all "illustrations of Christ's divine power and love in raising the *soul*, dead in trespasses and sins, from every kind of spiritual death, whether the soul be dead, but not yet carried out, like the daughter of Jairus; or dead and carried out, but not buried, like the widow's son; or dead, carried, and buried, like Lazarus."†

Augustine has something else to say. He writes, "He who raised himself from the dead can raise all from the death of sin. Therefore let no one despair."‡

The widow is a type of the Church. She has no husband here on earth, but she has children. She prays for them. The prophets intercede for her and join in her mourning. At last, the Lord Himself takes the place of her children upon the bier, and they are given back to their mother.

"Therefore let no one despair," says Augustine. Death is the wages of sin, but the poets and pundits who think it is inevitable or must

---

† St. Augustine, "Sermon" xcvii, quoted by Bishop Wordsworth, in *The Pulpit Commentary: St. Luke* Vol. 1, ed. H. D. M. Spence-Jones (Bellingham, WA: Logos Research Systems, Inc., 2004), p. 171.

‡ Ibid.

still be paid are wrong, dead wrong. Death has been swallowed up by death. What we now endure is not life, but living death. We are not the fortunate who yet suffer what we naively call "living." We are subhuman, not quite what we should be or what we were created to be because of our sins. And we are also only half alive. We are dying. Our bodies are failing, rushing toward the grave. We are rotting from inside out. The wages of sin and the justice of hell seek us through the years.

But Augustine says, "Let no one despair." What we call death is not death for those who have been washed in the blood of the Lamb and call upon His name. For them, death is a doorway to life. Blessed are the dead who die in the Lord. They are not dead. They live. For the death of Jesus Christ has been accepted on their behalf. He has taken their wages and taken the accuser's accusations. Justice is met and can ask no more. "He who raised himself from the dead can raise all from the death of sin."

Therefore, let no one, not even grieving widows, despair. The Lord has bought His Church with His own life. He has submitted to death to end death's tyranny. He has claimed you and your children and your loved ones for Himself and sealed them with His holy name in the waters of baptism.

Go ahead and mourn, you widows. Mourn for your husbands and mourn for your children. Mourn for the long years you must yet endure in this vale of tears without them. But do not mourn as those without hope. Jesus lives, and so do the husbands and children who have departed with the sign of faith. Those who sow in sorrow shall reap in joy. This separation is temporary. The reunion will not end.

St. Luke records how the widow was given back her son by the compassion and mercy of Jesus Christ, but he left off the end of the story. Because at some point, she was also given back her husband, never to be separated or to mourn again.

Lent is drawing down. Easter is coming. God be praised, He does all things well.

In ✠ Jesus' name. Amen.

Friday of Laetare

1 Kings 17:17-24
St. John 11:1-45

In the name of the Father and of the ✠ Son and of the Holy Spirit. Amen.

The resurrection of Lazarus is the fullest of the three resurrections recorded in the Gospels. It is also the closest parallel, and the more direct foreshowing, of our Lord's own resurrection. In this, of course, it is backwards. The Lord's resurrection gives rise to and defines Lazarus' resurrection, not the other way around. It is the same with the temple sacrifices. They came first in time, but it is our Lord's self-sacrifice on the cross that imputes grace to them.

We live in a backwards world. We see in a mirror dimly. We are often confused by our perspective from within time, even as we are corrupted by the sin that still clings to us. Jesus is the descendant of Abraham according to the flesh, but He precedes Abraham and is Abraham's Lord.

The Lord of Abraham is not confused even if we are. He has joined Himself to creation in time. He who has no beginning, but always is, began. He became flesh. Yet He remains united to His Father and to His Father's will. He is in no way confused, though He is humbled. For in this great exercise of His power, the taking up of our flesh in the Virgin's womb, He began to deny Himself. As a man, He did not always or fully use His divine rights and powers—until it was finished, and then He did. From the time of His resurrection until now, and forevermore, He always and fully uses His divine rights and powers as a man. But for a time, in time, He denied Himself in order to suffer all the things that we suffer and to keep the Law for us.

That is why He doesn't know certain things, such as the exact time of the end of the world or if there is some way for the cup to be lifted from Him on the night in which He is betrayed, not from confusion, but from humility and self-denial. He is not confused, but as a man, for a time, He is not omniscient. Still, He is not mistaken about the end. He simply denies Himself, as a man, the exact knowledge of all its details.

Still, even in His humility, He does sometimes, as a man, partially use His divine rights and powers. That is how He performs the miracles. And it is from that perspective that He can say to the disciples that the death of Lazarus is for the glory of God and that He is glad they weren't there to stop it. That is not just pious talk. He speaks with foresight. It probably doesn't make any sense to them, but they are stuck in time.

It is this same perspective that enables Him to rebuke Martha's pious-sounding words when she says, "I know that he will rise again in the resurrection on the last day." She is not wrong, but she is not right. She is faithful, but she is confused. She is confused by time.

She is piously holding to the true hope and expectation of the resurrection on the last day. But there is more to the promise of Christ Jesus than simply the future. He is present now. He walks the earth, on the lonely path to Jerusalem's gallows, as a man. He says to her, "I am the resurrection and the life." Present tense. "Whoever believes in me, though he die, yet shall he live, and everyone who lives and believes in me shall never die." Present tense with future consequence. "Do you believe this?"

Martha, thanks be to God, by the gift of the Holy Spirit, confesses, "Yes, I believe that Thou art the Christ."

That is the right answer in all difficulties, sorrow, and temptation: "I believe that Thou art the Christ." That is the right answer in confusion as well. "Do you believe that Lazarus, who is dead, is not dead? Do you believe that these evil things are for the glory of God, that it is good that Lazarus was not spared this pain, or you your grief?" He asks. And she says, "I believe that Thou art the Christ."

Jesus is the Christ. He is the resurrection and the life. That is the answer because it is the only thing that matters, the only thing that endures, the only thing that is trustworthy. Jesus is the Christ.

Yes, we can speculate and make up excuses and find ways that death is good or cancer is a gift, but it is pretty thin, and it rarely brings comfort. We do well to learn from St. Martha not to excuse the evil in this world, but to simply say, "I believe that Thou art the Christ. Somehow this will be good. I don't know how. I can't see it. But Thou art the Christ. I have a Savior. God loves me. Death itself will come to an end. Thou wilt bring it together and bring me home."

May God in His mercy keep this clearly in our hearts and minds, that whatever afflicts us—fear of death, despair of our sins, deep sadness and loneliness—we might be kept safe in this Word and faith until the end. Yes, I believe that Thou art the Christ.

In ✠ Jesus' name. Amen.

Saturday of Laetare

Isaiah 49:8-15
St. John 8:12-20

In the name of the Father and of the ✠ Son and of the Holy Spirit. Amen.

They loved darkness rather than light, but that did not keep them from understanding the claim of our Lord: "I am the light of the world." They knew, standing there in the court of the women, that He was claiming to be the Messiah, that He was the source of light and life in the world and would also redeem the world out of darkness. But since they loved darkness, they quoted a rabbinic law of evidence.

"No man can give witness of himself," they said. "But even if that were the case," says our Lord, "if I were giving witness of Myself alone, it would still be true." If the sun shining down upon the earth gives witness of itself, it does not become night. What He means is that even if His witness didn't fit their man-made rules, that didn't mean it wasn't true.

We can make the same application to formal logic. Something can be logically fallacious but still be true. For example, this is logically wrong: "Socrates is mortal, all men are mortal, so Socrates is a man." It is logically flawed because even though the premises are true—Socrates is mortal and men are mortal—they don't prove the conclusion. Socrates might be a dog. Dogs are mortal. So it doesn't work as a logical proof. Nonetheless, Socrates isn't a dog. He is a man, and he is a mortal. So the premises are true, and the conclusion is true even though the logic is flawed. God doesn't violate our logic—He and His Word are not illogical—but neither is He bound by it.

The same is true of the Law. The Lord doesn't violate the Law, but neither is He bound by it. What is true is true. Even if He gave witness of Himself, it would still be true. He is the light of the world. But He doesn't give testimony of Himself. The Jews ever want one more sign. The Gentiles ever want more proof, more wisdom and logic. They both refuse to acknowledge the testimony of the Baptist and the Scriptures and the Father. The prophecy of Abraham to the rich man is painfully true: "If they do not hear Moses and the prophets, neither will they be convinced if someone should rise from the dead" (Luke 16:31).

Repent. We've been the worst of the Jews and faithful to our pagan roots at the same time. We have sought to put the Holy Scriptures under a microscope, to stand judge over the Lord and His Word, to bend it to our purposes. We've ever sought more proof, more evidence, and more reasons while refusing the clear witness of Holy Scripture. That path leads to weeping and gnashing of teeth.

Despite us, the light shines in the darkness. All who receive His body and blood, who believe in His holy name, become children of God. You are born, not of blood nor of the will of the flesh nor of the will of man, but of God, in water and word and blood. He is not a destroying light. He is mercy.

Listen to the words of the psalmist:

> The Lord is my light and my salvation;
>   whom shall I fear?
> The Lord is the stronghold of my life;
>   of whom shall I be afraid? (Ps. 27:1)

Listen now to the prophet:

> The sun shall be no more
>   your light by day,
> nor for brightness shall the moon
>   give you light;
> but the Lord will be your everlasting light,
>   and your God will be your glory.
> Your sun shall no more go down,

nor your moon withdraw itself;
for the Lord will be your everlasting light,
and your days of mourning shall be ended. (Isa. 60:19-20)

This is what it means when the Lord stands in the court of the women and says, "I am the light of the world." Your days of mourning will end. The days of division between men and women, Jews and Gentiles, and even priest and laity will end. He promises, "I am the uniting, life-giving light who has paid the price of your salvation. Don't be afraid. Don't hide. The accusers have all departed, and I will not accuse you."

In ✠ Jesus' name. Amen.

The Fifth Sunday in Lent—Judica

Genesis 22:1-14
Hebrews 9:11-15
St. John 8:42-59

In the name of the Father and of the ✠ Son and of the Holy Spirit. Amen.

Since the beginning of Epiphany, we have been following our Lord in His ministry to the crowds and apostles. Now we begin to contemplate more directly the sorrowful happenings of the last year and week of His mortal life.

We see the hatred of His enemies increase by the day, about to break out on Good Friday in the most frightful of all crimes, in the vilest abuse of justice in all the sad history of man: the bloody drama of Calvary as foretold by the prophets and our Lord Himself.

The liturgy's accent of grief increases these next two weeks. We are now in what is called Passiontide. Already, the crosses have been veiled in mourning. The Gloria Patri has been taken away. Our hearts are overcast and penetrated with shame as we think on the price of our sins. The storm is rising, and it is not only the evil rabbis and the lustful mob that yell "crucify," it is also the Father who hates Jesus, whose wrath strikes out at the man made into a worm, the holy one who has become sin and a curse for the sake of His guilty brethren, for us. Who dares to think on such things?

The Lord Himself, the holy One, clothes Himself with our sins as with a garment. He was anointed in our filth, made to drink from our sewers, and has been thoroughly infected and dirtied as our Christ. The Lamb is slain, not a costly or unblemished sacrifice of the rich, not a bull, but a Lamb, beaten, bloody, cast down and despised, the offering for the poor. He is consumed and destroyed by heaven's justice and mercy, yet He makes not a single complaint. He is our Christ.

That is why He came to the temple, to the seat of mercy, to the house of prayer. He came to give proof of His divinity, to prepare Himself for the sacrifice. He addresses Himself with the divine name, and rather than falling down in worship, selfish men pick up stones to kill Him.

Abraham, the father of God's people, trusted in the divine promises of the Messiah. He longed and rejoiced to the see the day of the Messiah's incarnation and atonement. He saw it and rejoiced. Did He see it in the near sacrifice of Isaac and the providence of the ram caught in the thicket? He named that place not "The Lord has provided" but "The Lord will provide." Abraham saw more there than the temporary reprieve of Isaac. He saw the future.

The Lord provides in the temple built on that same mountain. He provided the ram, so also He provides on Golgotha the sacrifice in His only Son. Did Abraham see Good Friday in a vision or in some other prophecy or type, and rejoice? Or did he see it from heaven like unto Moses and Elijah at the transfiguration? I don't know. Perhaps the answer is all, or any, of the above. He saw it and rejoiced, that much we know. So too should we. We should rejoice in the death of Jesus Christ because it is that unjust death that causes Abraham and Isaac to live. They see and they rejoice.

I am afraid I have to drag you into some grammar here. It can't be helped. The Word became flesh. Grammar matters. In the first place, the name our Lord gives to Moses from the burning bush, "I am Who I am," is spoken in the first person. The Lord says, "I AM." That is His name. He is the One who is, the living and true God in contrast to all idols and all creatures. For everything that is, that moves and lives and has its being, only is by His power and at His mercy. Nothing else is. Pharaoh isn't. His gods aren't. And Moses isn't either. Neither are we. Only the Lord is. Thus He says, "I AM." But Moses immediately changes the name in Hebrew from "I AM" to "HE IS." He conjugates the verb. Moses isn't speaking of himself; he is speaking of the Lord.

So he doesn't say, "I AM," but "HE IS." The name Yahweh or Jehovah, which the Jews refused to say out loud, means "HE IS," third person, present tense.

Hold that thought. We'll come back to it.

The ESV and the KJV get the translation of Abraham's verb wrong. Our Lord does not use the past tense of the verb "is" for Abraham. He does not say before Abraham was, I WAS. He says that before Abraham came to be or was born, I AM. It is a subtle but important thing. The tense surprises us. We expect it to be "Before Abraham was, I was," meaning only that our Lord is older than Abraham, but it is worse than that. The tense and verb change, indicating our Lord's eternal character. He isn't born. He didn't come to be. Before Abraham was born, our Lord is. He always is. He never wasn't. He always will be.

But there is one more thing, that which caused them to pick up stones, and that which left them in no doubt at all what our Lord claimed for Himself. Perhaps you've already guessed it. When our Lord spoke, He didn't just use the name of Yahweh, or Jehovah, that the Jews refused to speak. He used the name spoken by God from the burning bush. He went one step worse than saying Yahweh. He didn't say what Moses said. He said what was heard by Moses from the bush. He said, "Ahweh," not "HE IS," but "I AM."

The Lord provides Himself for the sacrifice. He is the scapegoat, the peace offering, the whole burnt offering, the guilt offering, and the meal offering. He is the promise and the fulfillment. He is the Messiah. He comes in the temple to show Himself that He might fulfill all things and redeem mankind, whether mankind wants Him or not.

The liturgy is accented with grief, to be sure, for we are sinful men, full of vice, hatred, and lust. But the liturgy also hints at joy, expects with eagerness the king of glory who comes to save us. Lift up your heads; your redemption draws near. We have a high priest whose loves us, who wants us, who has established a new covenant in His blood that we might eat, drink, be cleansed, and have fellowship with Him.

In ✠ Jesus' name. Amen.

MONDAY IN PASSION WEEK

Jonah 3:1-10
St. John 7:32-39

In the name of the Father and of the ✠ Son and of the Holy Spirit. Amen.

St. Paul leaves no doubt that Christ is the rock, struck by Moses the Law-giver in anger, which followed the Israelites in the desert and provided them with water. Moses sins in anger over the sins of the people. Sin begets sin. Yet the anger of Moses delivers water to the people that neither he nor they deserve. This, however, is hardly surprising. It is typical of the history of men. We sin. God is gracious and provides. He is the God who works all things together for good, who uses what we meant for evil for our own good.

All men are thirsty without God, incomplete, dissatisfied, longing for that which they know not. Men were created by God to be righteous. To be in sin is to be like a hunting dog confined to a cage or a thoroughbred horse without legs. Why then do we think that sin will satisfy us? Repent.

All who thirst—that is, all men—should come unto Christ and be satisfied. He brings reconciliation with His Father, peace, and satisfaction. He is drank by faith, to be sure, but that faith is born and given in water and His name in Holy Baptism. Baptism makes of parched ground, of our souls, a watered garden, a cultivated and civilized place of peace.

Here is a surprise, though: "Whoever believes in me, as the Scripture has said, 'Out of his heart will flow rivers of living water." Christ applies a Messianic passage to the believers. Christ is the rock, but He dwells in our hearts. He joins Himself to us. And He flows out of us, out of the mouths of His preachers and the fonts of Christendom, to be sure, but also in the good works of His saints. You glorify the Father by glorifying the Son, by having your sins forgiven and confessing His holy name. You are the reward and booty given to the Son and you are pleasing, delightful, to God in Christ. Thus your works are good and extend the kingdom on earth.

> You will say in that day:
> "I will give thanks to you, O Lord,
> for though you were angry with me,
> your anger turned away,
> that you might comfort me.
>
> "Behold, God is my salvation;
> I will trust, and will not be afraid;
> for the Lord God is my strength and my song,
> and he has become my salvation."
>
> With joy you will draw water from the wells of salvation.
> And you will say in that day:
>
> "Give thanks to the Lord,
> call upon his name,
> make known his deeds among the peoples,
> proclaim that his name is exalted." (Isa. 12:1-4)

All the Scriptures testify of the Christ. All of the Old Testament is Messianic. But there is more because all the Messianic passages are rightly applied to those in whom the Messiah dwells, those to whom the Spirit has been given. The Bible is your book. That is why it rings so true. It is about you and how God has bent all of time and creation to rescue and save you.†

In ✠ Jesus' name. Amen.

---

† This sermon is dependent, in part, upon the notes for Passiontide and Passion Sunday provided from St. Leo and St. Gregory in *the St. Andrew Daily Missal* as republished by St. Bonaventure Publications in 1999. www.libers.com

Tuesday in Passion Week

Daniel 14:28-42
St. John 7:1-13

In the name of the Father and of the ✠ Son and of the Holy Spirit. Amen.

The Church is taking us backwards. On Sunday, we heard of our Lord's encounter in the temple from John 8. Yesterday, we moved back to the end of John 7. Today, we go back yet again, to the first part of John 7.

The Church knows that we know the story. We are well familiar with the betrayal in the garden and the trial. We know how He is executed and who is there. And we know of His resurrection, for we do not eat and drink the dead body and blood of Christ, but even as we proclaim His death in each communion, we proclaim as well that He lives. We eat and drink the risen body and blood of Christ. So the Church does not need to give us a historical re-enactment, a passion play, or a chronological accounting, and she doesn't. What she does is seek to put us in mind of the details and to enlighten Scripture with Scripture. She does this deliberately with the daily propers, as verses and psalms, Old Testament readings, selections from the Epistles, and pieces of the Holy Gospels are placed side by side. But she does it seasonally also. She is preparing us for heaven by preparing us to celebrate Easter. Today she places the great events of our Lord's passion in context that we would remember the acts and arguments that He endured.

But, of course, it is even greater than that, for the context of our Lord's death and resurrection is not simply His life and ministry since the incarnation. It is also Daniel in the lion's den, Susanna's suffering of false accusations, and the near sacrifice of Isaac. So also the context includes the burning bush, the parting of the Red Sea, and the giving of the Law. What we learn is that we sinners and the devil have made the earth hostile to God at all points, for the context is also our own betrayals and failures, our sins. We would make ourselves His enemies.

For six months, the Lord had walked in Galilee. He knew that the authorities sought to kill Him. He knew that even His own brothers did not believe in Him. He went as a lamb to the slaughter, silent, but not ignorant. He knew what was in store. We might look upon the sad scene in Bethlehem and think it nostalgic, but it was not so for Him. He was rejected from the first and never found a place to lay His head until He laid it upon the holy cross.

And when we did feign some hospitality, He rejected it. He did not accept the compliments of Nicodemus, for He is more than a teacher or a rabbi. Nor He did accept the praise of the crowds, for He is more than a prophet or miracle worker. If you will call Him Messiah, Christ, then you must know what it means. He is the Lord, the creator, the sustainer, the giver. He is Yahweh, the great I AM, who comes as suffering servant and ransom. If He is not this, then He is nothing. And if you will not have Him as this, King-Messiah come as Creator-Redeemer, then you will not have Him at all.

Yet despite the hostility, He would not quit. We, in vanity, sought to be His enemies, but He declared us His friends and children. He has laid down His life to redeem and rescue us from hell. And the prince of this world, death, and hell do not want to lose their prize. They are His enemy, and they seek to keep us with them. They seethe with anger and jealousy. But He comes to rescue and redeem and take what is His. They cannot have us.

May God in His mercy send angels to grab us by the hair and take us to the holy cross, to gaze upon love in the flesh, love giving everything to have us, pouring out blood and water for us to drink and be cleansed. May God keep us from ever taking this for granted or forgetting!

Let us zoom out today and place the passion in context. Let us go back to John 7, back to Daniel, back to the Garden of Eden. The Church would show us the big picture and our place in it. There we see this consistent reality: We are sinful, but the Lord is merciful. In that light, the crucifixion is no surprise, but it remains, somehow, still surprising. Yes, this is the way God has always been to and for us: He keeps on in the face of hostility and His mercy endures forever. He sows. We reap. He gives. We take. He pours out His blood and we drink. God be praised.

In ✠ Jesus' name. Amen.

WEDNESDAY IN PASSION WEEK

Leviticus 19:1-2, 11-19a, 25b
St. John 10:22-38

In the name of the Father and of the ✠ Son and of the Holy Spirit. Amen.

The Lord is at the temple, walking, in the winter, and the Jews in the midst of partying are cold. We see again something of St. John's storytelling ability. They circle Him like bees and feign some piety. "Tell us plainly," they say, "whether Thou art the Christ. For Thou hast caused us to doubt"—literally, lifted our souls from us—"for too long."

It is winter, and the earth seems dead. These men do not want an answer. They do not seek in piety. They are bored and cold. They want some sport. He has plainly said that He is the Messiah often enough for those with ears to hear. So also do His miracles and life attest to the same: He is the Christ.

They are not doubting; they are unbelieving. There is a difference. The children of God, His own sheep, suffer doubt in this fallen life. All of us live with two minds, one faithful to God and one that pesters and hounds and mocks us. These men have no doubt. They have only winter boredom and hate.

In the face of this growing hostility, our Lord's tenderness shines forth. They do not deserve these kind words, nor do we. But here is what He says:

> My sheep hear my voice, and I know them, and they follow me. I give them eternal life, and they will never perish, and no one will snatch them out of my hand. My Father, who has given them to me, is greater than all, and

no one is able to snatch them out of the Father's hand. I
and the Father are one. (John 10:27-30)

The people of Jerusalem are like sheep without shepherds. The rabbis have turned on them, abandoned the Messianic hope of sacrifice.
The priests are servants of Caesar and of their own bellies. They do not
want the Messiah. They want only the status quo, only living for the
moment, unable to see what truly ails them. They do not think they
need a Physician, a Shepherd, or a Lord. And the Lord looks upon them
with compassion.

Despite these evil men of the City of Peace, there in Jerusalem His
flock will hear His voice on Palm Sunday. The faithful will cry out,
"Hosanna, save us." He will accept their praise and worship. For them,
He, the stone that the builders rejected, will go to the cross to be their
Savior, that they would have a good and faithful Shepherd.

They hear His voice but, like us, they are easily misled and confused.
It is likely that some of those who cried "Hosanna" on Sunday cried
"crucify" on Friday, even as some of us cry "Hosanna" this morning and
then proceed to hate our lives or despise our children or lust for women
not our wives. The builders pick up stones to kill the Messiah, to put an
end to His reign through violence. The sheep are scattered once again.

Sheep without a shepherd, chicks without a mother, builders who
choose their own material and reject the divine: This is humanity without the Christ. But the Shepherd is persistent. He never wavers. He
walks in the temple, in Solomon's porch, in the winter, showing Himself despite the danger. He knows we need Him. He knows we are weak.
He will not quit. He seeks the lost sheep of the house of Israel, even
those who must be made sons of Abraham by faith. They—Jews and
Gentiles alike—hear His voice and follow Him and receive eternal life.

Why else are you here? You have heard His voice. You have come
to the sheepfold for fodder, for daily bread to feed your soul. You have
heard His voice and have been given eternal life. No evil rabbi, corrupt

president, or lying pastor can snatch you away. Nor can your doubts, fears, or sins conquer His seeking love.

In ✠ Jesus' name. Amen.

Thursday in Passion Week

Daniel 3:25, 34-45
St. Luke 7:36-50

In the name of the Father and of the ☩ Son and of the Holy Spirit. Amen.

Who is this who forgives sins? It is the prophet like Moses, who is not only a prophet but is also a priest forever in the order of Melchizedek and is the heir to the throne of heaven. He is Jacob's ladder, upon whom the angels ascend and descend. He is the kinsman-redeemer seen long ago by the soon-to-decay eyes of Job back from the dead. He is the suffering servant, the sacrificial Lamb, the mercy seat of the Lord that stands between us and the Law.

Simon the Pharisee is interested in Jesus, but for all the wrong reasons. The penitent woman, who had found grace, acceptance, and mercy in Jesus, is not just interested; she is in love. Having received so great a gift, even life itself, she cannot contain herself. Her joy overflows. Her tears wet the dusty, grimy feet not yet pierced. She wipes them with her hair, brushes them with her lips, and anoints them with oil. How beautiful are the feet of Him who brings good news, who proclaims peace, who brings glad tidings of good things, who proclaims salvation, who says to Zion, "Your God reigns!"

The good news those feet brought is that our God reigns by the death and resurrection of Jesus Christ. He rules over His children by the power of forgiveness in the kingdom of grace. His love declares them righteous. That is what causes the sinful, penitent woman to weep. We suspect that she is Mary from Magdala, from whom seven demons were cast out, who was faithful at the foot of the cross, and who first saw the risen Lord. But here Simon notes that she is a sinner. Indeed, Simon, and that is to her benefit. For the Lord only receives and eats with sinners.

Her confession and penance are courageous, bold, and unashamed because her God reigns. She does not care what Simon, or anyone else, thinks of her. She knows what Christ thinks of her, esteeming her high enough to die for, by means of the most shameful and excruciating death known to man. Mary—and let's just go ahead and call her Mary—by the grace of God in Christ Jesus, is finished defending herself, looking out after herself, holding grudges and prejudices, fighting for everything she has. She no longer boasts or postures. She is not being provocative or seductive. She is empty of bravado and pride and worry. Her heart is open. She is free. She lets go.

She has heard her Shepherd's voice. She has found perfect joy and liberty in the wounds of the risen Lord, for that voice has called her from the bondage to sin, from the seduction of death. It has found and restored her. It has cleansed and purified her. In Him, by Him, she is blameless and chaste. She is immaculate, and Simon who thinks himself clean is filthy. Her heart and eyes overflow at the goodness that is God whose feet catch her tears.

Oh no, Simon doesn't like it, not one bit. Jesus doesn't fit with the kind of god that Simon wants. Jesus is too much, too extreme, too radical. Simon wants a more conventional, convenient, and comfortable god. He is embarrassed by Jesus and Mary. He becomes defensive and judgmental. What kind of prophet is this!

What kind, indeed, Simon? Is it so shocking to think that He might be a Moses kind of prophet, a Hosea who comes from unfaithful Gomer, a God who forgives and loves sinners? Could it be, Simon, that He is more than a prophet and exactly what you need?

But what of us? How often have we tried to apologize for God to modern Simons because God did not behave in ways that pleased them or us? How often have we been ashamed that God is so uncompromising, so unbending when it comes to "modern" issues like women's ordination, homosexuality, or fornication? How have the Simons of our day chided us with their damning remarks? Have we not heard, again and again, "What kind of a god would allow..." and then fill in your tragedy or injustice: the Holocaust, Columbine, or even the near-extinction of pandas?

Repent. This is no game. We are not in control, and we do not get to judge God. God does not answer to us. He is God. We are not. His ways are not our ways. His thoughts are not our thoughts. But He is good. His mercy does endure forever. He does seek and save, cleanse and restore, forgive and love. He does all things well. Ours is not to reason why. Ours is just to believe, to throw ourselves upon His mercy, to suffer the scolding and shame of Simon and the Pharisees that we would gain the love of Christ.

Mysterious and unexpected as it is, He cleanses and purifies sinners, even the most horrible and notorious of sinners. He heals them by the power of His atoning, sacrificial, life-giving, life-preserving death and resurrection. He feeds and nourishes them with the fruit of that holy death: His body and blood. He names them with His name. He welcomes and comforts them. He has freely, from His own sovereignty, forgiven them.

What manner of God is this? It is the God of mercy, the God of Abraham, Isaac, and Jacob, the God who satisfied His own wrath to rescue us from hell. His name is Jesus, for He saves His people. God be praised for Mary! And may He give us the strength and charity, the courage and conviction, to follow her example. But most of all, God be praised that He has even forgiven us.

In ✠ Jesus' name. Amen.

FRIDAY IN PASSION WEEK

Jeremiah 17:13-18
St. John 11:47-54

In the name of the Father and of the ✠ Son and of the Holy Spirit. Amen.

In John 11, where Caiaphas first makes the prophecy we heard again today in the passion, the fear of the Sanhedrin is not that Jesus is an imposter. What they fear is that He really is the Messiah. The rabbis of the previous generations had studied the Scriptures. They taught that the birth of the Messiah would cause the destruction of the temple and Jerusalem and that the Messiah would gather all people, even Gentiles, into one nation. So if Jesus is a fake, no problem. But if He is the Messiah, their way of life will come to an end.

They are aware of this reality as they gather in council and fulfill the prophesy of Psalm 2. But most of them are not bold enough to say what is really at stake. They skirt around it. It is as though they say, "Look at what this man does. He might be the Messiah! What then must we do? It would be evil to kill Him, and, if we did, the crowds might rebel against us. But we cannot abide Him, and if we do nothing, all men will believe on Him. What can we do?"

Caiaphas then answers, "You know nothing. Whether He is the Messiah or not does not matter because it is expedient—it is necessary—that He should die rather than the whole nation should perish."

Caiaphas did not say this from himself, that is, according to faith. He said it according to his holy office, not as a prophet but as the high priest, the one who offers sacrifices. His office is to kill innocent animals as a substitute for the people, to push the sins of the people down into the scapegoat and then banish him to the wilderness and death. All of this was understood by the previous generations as foreshowing the cross. So Caiaphas, even though he means it for evil, speaks in perfect accord with the Holy Spirit and the fathers. It is, in fact, good, right, and in every way salutary that the Messiah die for the nation, that He be offered to the Father as the holocaust and peace offering and thereby gather the children of God from the four corners of the earth into one. Herein is the entire hope of the Old Testament.

Now, St. John gives us this in an especially delicious way. Because Caiaphas doesn't say, "It is expedient or profitable that He should die rather than the whole of Israel," but he says for the whole of the *ethnos*. That is the Greek word that means Gentiles. The nation that is saved by the death of the Messiah is not the nation-state of Israel. It is the whole of humanity. And indeed, if an ethnic son of Abraham, even Caiaphas himself, would be saved, he must become as a Gentile.

Now, as I already said, the great expectation of the Jews before Christ was that the Christ would gather together Israel, the *diaspora*, and the Gentiles into one people, one *ethnos*. The council, in league with Satan, despairs that Jesus, should He live, could do this very thing. That was supposed to be their hope and expectation, but they despair of it.

And then it twists. They expected that if Jesus lived, He would gather the children of God into one. But, in fact, He accomplishes this not by living, but by dying, and that, at their hand.

They believed their religion established the nation of God, but the actual establishment of that nation was by sacrifice, by grace, and was of all people, Jew and Gentile, as it had been from the beginning. They thought to secure themselves by the death of Christ when, in fact, it is that very death, that holy sacrifice, that overthrows their religion, power, and nation. The Christ secures only those who cannot secure themselves.

They should have known better, but such is the foolishness of sin and hardened hearts. Day after day they slaughtered the sacrifices and yet became blind to the very character of their office and the gifts and purpose of the temple.

The sacrifice and resurrection of the Messiah bestows the kingdom upon Gentiles and likewise upon those Jews willing to be as Gentiles and heathen. Jesus only eats with and receives sinners. No one enters this kingdom by right or by birth. It cannot be inherited. Nicodemus must be born from above, no matter who his earthly mother is. No one has the right pedigree. So everyone who comes into the kingdom comes by grace and receives it as a gift, or not at all.

This is our greatest benefit and profit: The Lord Jesus Christ has been betrayed, treated spitefully and abused, handed over to the Gentiles and killed, so that we would not only not die but also so that we would be gathered together into the new Israel and have fellowship with God.

Thank you, Caiaphas. You have done us a better turn than the brothers of Joseph. What you meant for evil is our greatest, our most expedient, good. You have offered the one sacrifice we so desperately needed, the sacrifice that makes us His and gathers us to Him.

Thanks be to God. He does all things well. Easter draws near.

In ✝ Jesus' name. Amen.

Saturday in Passion Week

Jeremiah 18:18-23
St. John 12:10-36

In the name of the Father and of the ✠ Son and of the Holy Spirit. Amen.

All of Holy Week is foreshown in St. John's account of Palm Sunday.

The Lord enters Jerusalem to the worshipful request of the pious: "Hosanna, save us." But within a few days some of those sheep without a shepherd, betrayed by evil rabbis and priests, will cry out "crucify." He will be lifted up from the earth, separated from the love of His Father, roasted whole in holy wrath and the hatred of hell. Good Friday casts its shadow over all of His short life, but it is particularly dark in the week before He dies.

The Greeks here who come to Philip represent the Gentile fruit that comes from the Lord's falling to the earth and rising again. It is expedient that this man die, that a new nation be formed. The Gentiles do not see Jesus apart from His death, nor do they see Him as long as they love their own lives. But the Son of Man is lifted up from the earth on that cruel scaffold to draw all things, even Gentiles, unto Himself. The resurrection, Easter, is the light behind the cross that casts the shadow. Like the shadow of St. Peter, this shadow heals, or rather, more correctly said, the shadow of St. Peter heals like this and on account of this.

This proclamation on Palm Sunday, "[U]nless a grain of wheat falls into the earth and dies, it remains alone; but if it dies, it bears much fruit," troubles our Lord's soul. He is the grain that will be lifted up from the earth and then fall to the earth and sealed in an earthen tomb. His sorrow and His explanation of what is coming foreshows

Gethsemane: "For this purpose I have come to this hour. Father, glorify your name." The Father speaks from heaven and comforts the Son even as He will send angels in Gethsemane.

He is lifted up from the earth, of course, on Good Friday. He becomes not just sin and a curse for our sake, but also a worm. He is a worm, a snake, a dragon, and no man. His effigy was lifted up in the desert, and the people who looked upon it were saved. Now He who knew no sin, who obeyed His Father in all ways, who loves His neighbor as Himself without caveat or limit, is lifted up from the earth, away from creation, away from the goodness of God, and forsaken, despised, stricken, smitten, and afflicted.

Would you see Jesus, O Greek? See Him there. There is your Lord. There is love. There is hope. There, on the cross, is God and salvation.

There is sadness in this, to be sure. But there is also Easter. The grain of wheat falls to the earth and is buried, but it does stay there. It rises and bears fruit, much fruit. The sacrifice is terrible but not outside of time. It comes to an end. It is finished, and Jesus rises from the dead.

May God give us the strength and courage to not look away this week but to rejoice in the vision of that which has saved us. The Father has glorified the name of Jesus by placing it upon us.

In ✠ Jesus' name. Amen.

Palm Sunday

Zechariah 9:9-12
Philippians 2:5-11
St. Matthew 21:1-9

In the name of the Father and of the ✠ Son and of the Holy Spirit. Amen.

The date palm was among the earliest cultivated trees. They are characteristic of oases and watered places, and their fruit is edible. The judge Deborah rendered her decisions under a palm tree, and the Hebrew poets counted the palm as a symbol of beauty and prosperity. Palms were used in the construction of the booths for the festival of booths, and carved images of palms were used by divine command to decorate the temple.

Not everyone in Jerusalem may have known all this. Whether they did or not, it seems likely that at least some of those who cry, "Hosanna to the Son of David," were confused about what was happening or where Jesus was going. But the saints in heaven, washed in the blood of the Lamb, were not. St. John, in his vision of the apocalypse, sees palms in the hands of those who have come through the great tribulation and have been washed in the blood of the Lamb. They take up palms to identify with our Lord's entry into Jerusalem as a sacrifice. They rejoice to see the real victory, not a military hero or a great visionary but the sacrifice who rode on to redeem them despite the terrible cost.

Palm branches represent an oasis, water and food, rest and shelter, in a barren and hostile place. This is what God gives in the temple and in His Word: He gives refreshment, rest, safety. Jesus is the temple built without hands. He abides in the hearts of the faithful. He enters into them through His sacrificed, yet risen, body and blood. So the saints in heaven decorate themselves like the temple on earth, with palms, for they are the place of the Lamb's gracious blood, the temples of the Holy Spirit.

This is why we also can take up palms. We are yet in the great tribulation. We are still attacked by the devil, the world, and our fallen nature. Yet we are one with them, the great cloud of witnesses, our brothers who have gone before us in the sign of faith. We too are temples of the Holy Spirit. We too identify with our Lord's victory in death. So we take palms.

That doesn't mean every one of us has understood this perfectly, either now or in years past. We might yet be confused, only dipping our toes into the waters rather than swimming. In that, we are like some of the crowd on Palm Sunday, even the holy apostles themselves. We may not fully understand the significance of palms or kneeling or the chants, but that is okay. The kingdom comes by grace, not by understanding. You have a lifetime and beyond to enjoy and to learn these things.

But worse yet, we may not fully understand what the Lord Jesus has done for us in allowing them to do those terrible things to Him. We may not understand why He rode that Sunday and how He answered the cry, "Hosanna." We can never fully solve these mysteries here on earth, but we do well to apply our hearts to wisdom and to contemplate these holy things. Let us do so and thus prepare for Holy Week.

First, we need to remember that our God, the Lord Jesus, rode to His death on the cross as a man. He took up our cause and has taken our very nature to the cross. Human nature, fallen and corrupt, was under the wrath of God. It was impossible for men to find favor with God in this state. The Scriptures teach that all "were by nature the children of wrath" (Eph. 2:3), "by the deeds of the law there shall no flesh be justified" (Rom. 3:20 KJV), and the "wicked shall be turned into hell, and all the nations that forget God" (Ps. 9:17 KJV).

This is what the Christ took up: our flesh of wrath. He took it that He might do and suffer what was impossible for us. He carried it, our nature, through His earthly days as a life of penance. He carried it in agony, suffering in all the ways we suffer, until He submitted, at last, even to death. In Him, our sinful nature died and rose again. It died on the cross and was buried. Yet that death was its new creation. In Christ, it satisfied its old and heavy debt. For in Him, our nature was without sin. He had kept it pure. He had kept the Law. Thus, when it had been offered up upon the cross and was made perfect by suffering, our nature in the Christ became the first-fruits of a new man and was restored to its place in creation and beyond.

He did not sin; the Law was fulfilled. He was not a child of wrath, but He allowed the Law to do to Him everything that the Law demanded of Law-breakers. He was declared a child of wrath and was not spared any of hell's fury or sin's shame. Again: The Law was fulfilled. It had nothing left to accuse us with. It was spent all upon Him. Our nature, in Christ, was clean once again. He was declared a sinner. He paid the wages demanded by justice, and you are declared righteous and holy and receive the wages of mercy.

Thus, St. Paul writes that if one died for all, then *all* died (2 Cor. 5:14); our old man is crucified *in Him*, that the *body* of sin might be destroyed (Rom. 6:6); and together with Christ when we were dead in sins, He quickened us, and raised us up together, and made us sit together in heavenly places in Christ Jesus (Eph. 2:5-6).

We are now members of his body (Eph. 5:30), from His flesh, and from His bones. For whosoever eats His flesh and drinks His blood has eternal life. His flesh is meat indeed, and His blood is drink indeed. He that eats His flesh and drinks His blood dwells in Him, and He in him (John 6:54-56).†

This is why the angels and perfected saints rejoice this week and hold their palms. Let us do the same and mingle our praise with theirs.

In ✠ Jesus' name. Amen.

---

† The section that begins "Human nature, fallen and corrupt, was under the wrath of God," until the footnote is modified from a sermon by John Henry Newman found in *Parochial and Plain Sermons, Volume 6* (London; Oxford; Cambridge: Rivingtons, 1868), pp. 79-80.

HOLY MONDAY

Isaiah 50:5-10
1 Peter 3:21-24
St. John 12:1-43

In the name of the Father and of the ✠ Son and of the Holy Spirit. Amen.

Jesus is in the house of Lazarus, at dinner, six days before the Passover, the day before Palm Sunday. St. Mary approaches and anoints His feet for burial, then she tenderly dries them with her hair. Judas resents her action and resolves upon his evil course.

These two noteworthy characters, Mary of Bethany and Judas, produce a powerful effect by way of contrast. Together they typify our relation to the Christ: He gives His body to Magdalenes to be anointed, and He gives it likewise to Judases to be kissed. He gives Himself to good persons who repay Him with love and service, and He gives Himself to foes who crucify Him. We, of course, have been—and are—both. We are Mary, and we are Judas. We are saint, and we are sinner.

How well this is expressed in the reading assigned from Isaiah: "I gave my back to the smiters, and my cheeks to them that plucked off the hair: I hid not my face from shame and spitting" (KJV).

We must apply this to ourselves. This is not a story about other people. This is the account of our lives. In all Christian hearts dwell two souls: a Judas-soul and a Mary-soul, an old man and a new man. The old man must be beaten down and subdued by daily contrition and repentance, that the new man may emerge by grace to live before God in the forgiveness that declares him pure and holy.

The Mary-soul, the new man who longs to anoint and kiss the feet that bring good news from God, the feet that are nailed to the tree of life for us, is encouraged and strengthened by God's Word and

Sacrament. She rejoices in the path that the Lord has chosen and the chalice that He drinks for her. Indeed, the hour is now come. The Son of Man is glorified by being lifted up from the earth. If you would see Him, if you would behold Jesus, behold Him there. There, and there alone, you might gaze upon God's glory and not be destroyed, for you gaze upon where and how He was destroyed for you. There you might look into the things that the prophets longed to see and kings desired. There you will know the love God holds for you and the cost He has gladly paid to make you His.

But we speak not only metaphorically, for we believe that the blind see by hearing. Hear the Word of God. Hear the account of His holy death and resurrection this week and therein see Jesus. There, in the inspired account of His suffering and death, God reveals Himself to His children. So also, there is some seeing by faith when the eyes behold the bread and faith confesses that it is the body of Christ. That is why, having beheld Christ in the Sacrament, we sing even with Simeon, "Mine eyes have seen thy salvation."

Would you see Jesus? Would you anoint and kiss His feet? Then hear His holy passion and see Him upon the cross. Receive His body and blood in the Sacrament where He gives Himself to and for you.†

In ✠ *Jesus' name. Amen.*

---

† This sermon has taken some ideas and vocabulary from Pius Parsch's words on Holy Monday as found in volume 2 of Parsch, Pius, *The Church's Year of Grace*: Vol. 1-4. Tr. Rev. William G. Heidt. (Collegeville, MN: The Liturgical Press, 1964).

Holy Tuesday

Jeremiah 11:18-20
1 Timothy 6:12-14
St. Mark 14:1-15:47

In the name of the Father and of the ✠ Son and of the Holy Spirit. Amen.

Yesterday we heard the reading from St. Peter: "He himself bore our sins in his body on the tree, that we might die to sin and live to righteousness. By his wounds you have been healed. For you were straying like sheep, but have now returned to the Shepherd and Overseer of your souls" (1 Pet. 2:24-25).

The word St. Peter used, which is translated "stripes" in the KJV or "wounds" in the ESV, is actually singular. It is the word for welt or wound. The Roman lash was a mop head of leather straps embedded with bits of bone and metal. Our Lord's back wasn't striped with many different cuts. It was one giant, open wound. Even if they hadn't crucified Him, it is fairly certain that He would have died from the lashes.

What sort of evil could cause one man to do this to another? No man, no matter how evil, would do this to a dog or any animal. And then—having opened His back in this way so that He is bleeding and dying and in total agony in front of you—to take Him to the barracks, slap Him, and push down a crown of thorns upon His head, how is that even possible?

The cruelty here baffles even the selfish and cruel Pilate. He sees through the pettiness of the priests. He recognizes their motives and he, veteran of Rome's brutal legions, is moved to something akin to pity. He does not know that Jesus is the Messiah, God in the flesh, but he knows the priests are evil and Jesus is no threat. Yet look how the crowd rallies for blood. Sadly, the priests are better politicians than Pilate, and his pity is sorely lacking. The priests may have been transparent to him, but that didn't keep them from manipulating him. He should have heeded the advice of his wife. Kyrie Eleison!

So Barabbas goes free, and Jesus is condemned. Barabbas is a generic sort of name, which means "son of the father." He is a known insurrectionist and murderer. In modern terms, we would call him a terrorist, but even that is almost too tame. He is a child pornographer, a serial killer, a rapist, the cause and perpetrator of the Holocaust, and a killer of pandas and baby seals. He is whatever is most repulsive in mankind.

In contrast, Jesus is a known healer and giver of food in the wilderness. Even when they accused Him of having a demon, they themselves didn't believe it. Everyone knows that Jesus is good, but they demand He be executed because He claims to be the Messiah, and that supposedly false claim makes Him a threat to Caesar. Yet they insist that Barabbas, the man proven to be a threat to Caesar, be freed.

How can Pilate have no courage against them? What sort of a governor releases a terrorist and executes a man who is, at worst, a harmless kook? The Pilate-sort, that's who. He gives in to their evil desires. Water, without the Word, will not wash his hands clean. Regret without faith will see him to hell.

The Church, however, has long had traditions and legends concerning both Barabbas and Pilate. It is not surprising, really. Both witnessed the grace of Christ's sacrifice. Especially since they were both so directly involved, it has been thought that the Holy Spirit moved in these events and created faith in both of them. With Barabbas it is particularly obvious. Christ died as his substitute in both the courts of heaven and Caesar. He doesn't die under Pilate as justice demanded. Neither does he die eternally in hell as justice likewise demanded. Pilate's rehabilitation also makes a kind of sense when considered according to the character of grace. Like unto St. Stephen's forgiveness of those who stoned him, what could be more fitting than Pilate being washed with water and the Word, and being given not simply a second chance but the benefit of Christ's sacrifice, for which he was directly responsible but which was also for his benefit?

It is a strange story, full of sad events, but in this way the Scripture is fulfilled. Satan is cast out. The cherubim guarding paradise are removed. Here is the great mystery: The evil lust of the crowd and the will of the Father are one. The Father and the Son desire that the thief go to paradise, that sinners be offered a place in heaven and become sons of the Father by grace. The beloved Son was willing to give up His rightful place to make room for them and for you. The Father forsook the Son for Barabbas, for Pilate, for Caiaphas. He forsook the Son for you.

In ✝ *Jesus' name. Amen.*

HOLY WEDNESDAY

Isaiah 62:11-63:7
Isaiah 53:1-12
St. Luke 22:1-23:56

In the name of the Father and of the ✠ Son and of the Holy Spirit. Amen.

The centurion, seeing what had happened, praised God and said, "Surely this was a righteous man."

Martin Luther wrote, "The right way to reach a true knowledge of Christ's sufferings is to perceive and understand not only what He suffered, but how it was His heart and will to suffer. For whoever looks upon Christ's sufferings without seeing His heart and will therein must be filled with fear rather than joy, but if we can truly see His heart and will in it, it gives true comfort, trust, and joy in Christ."†

Here we see laid bare the problem that some have with the cross. They fail to see the heart and will of Christ. Our focus should not be on the agony and pain that our Lord endured. The focus should be, as it is in the Bible, on our Lord's free and loving desire to bear our sins in His own body to death on the cross.

And if you cannot bear the thought of the cross, then you are not a Christian. If you will not have the crucified Lord, then you do not have the Lord. If you want something nicer, something kinder, something gentler, then Satan has alternatives galore for your perusal. He will gladly hold your hand on the broad, easy path to hell. But if you would be saved, you must overcome the stumbling block of the cross, the scandal of Jesus' death; rather, you must be overcome by it.

---

† Sermon from the year 1525. W.A. 17. II.173 f. translated at www.standrewslaramie.org/divineservice/churchyear/prelent/quinquagesima/luther.html

Thus the centurion, as recorded by St. Luke, saw what had happened, and he praised God. Seeing the kind of death that Jesus died, the centurion praised God. This is not the sentiment of General George Patton, looking upon the men he sacrificed for victory and urging us not to bemoan the fact that such men died, but to "thank God that such men lived."† Rather, this soldier recognizes that this wasn't his sacrifice to win some victory, but God's sacrifice to win him.

So he gets neither gloomy nor triumphant. He is not filled with terror, horror, or guilt, nor is He self-satisfied. After sinking his spear into our Lord's blessed side and setting free the water and the blood, he praises God, saying, "Surely this was a righteous man. Surely this man was the Son of God!" And that is something to praise God about. For if Jesus Christ is the righteous Son of God, then payment has been rendered for the unrighteous sons of the devil—that is to say, for us.

Jesus, then, is more than a martyr. His death is more than noble. There is joy at His death, not because He stood up for a cause or was brave or even did the right thing. Rather, there is joy in His death because this is the atoning sacrifice for all the world and is the heart and will of the Father. This is not simply the death of an innocent man who loved His brothers. This is the great injustice and intervention of God Himself. God lays down His life for His enemies. Patton's soldiers died at his command and will for their country. Jesus died of His own will for His enemies. If Patton's soldiers had done that, we would call them traitors.

Gathered about the cross that Good Friday, only the repentant thief and the centurion really get it. The majority there—even the inner circle of the disciples, Mary Magdalene, and the blessed virgin—all beat their breasts and mourn over the sad fact of these three crucifixions. They see no glory, no power, no love of God there, but only another human tragedy.

---

† Speech at the Copley Plaza Hotel, Boston, MA (7 June 1945), quoted in Patton: Ordeal and Triumph (1970) by Ladislas Farago.

But the centurion, seeing the kind of death Jesus died, recognizes, by the grace of God, who Jesus is. He rejoices and praises God. For the death of Jesus Christ is substitutionary. It was not a soldier's death or a martyr's death. It was sin's death, and if Jesus seems a bit like a traitor, so be it. For He opened heaven to traitors. The centurion recognizes that Jesus has died in his place, that Jesus has substituted His perfect life and death for his. He realizes that he could not have obtained this in any other way. In his sins, he was God's sworn and eternal enemy, but Jesus died for him, to make him the friend and even the bride of God. So he praises God.

Let us join him. We have no less to praise God for than he did. We too have been born anew in the water and blood set free by his spear; we too have been made the friends and bride of God. This is truly something for which to praise God, for surely this Jesus is a righteous man for us, and by His righteousness we are declared righteous. Surely He is the Son of God, who makes us His brothers and thereby also sons of God. Surely His death is our salvation and His resurrection is the inauguration, the beginning, the breaking out of our own future resurrections. The Son of Man has been lifted up on the cruel killing scaffold, and it is the tree of life. This event has drawn us to Him. It is a good day, the best day, the day the Lord has made, the day He made us His.

Praise God, Jesus died to make us free. Praise God, He did not shrink from His mission but loved us to the end. Praise God, He is not dead. He lives, and we too live in Him. Our "Hallelujahs" draw nigh. Easter is coming.

In ✠ Jesus' name. Amen.

MAUNDY THURSDAY

Exodus 12:1-14
1 Corinthians 11:23-32
St. John 13:1-15

In the name of the Father and of the ✠ Son and of the Holy Spirit. Amen.

When God bound up the future of all nations in the history of Abraham and his Seed, He made that history prophetic. Each event and every rite of Israel became flower buds on a tree. Each bud, each law, each ceremony, as beautiful as it was, was temporary, destined to blossom as a flower and then to ripen into fruit. That fruit is the cross of Jesus Christ, the culmination of all history, the gift of God to man, and under the shadow of the cross all nations are gathered and made the sons of God.†

Of all those rites and in all that varied history of grace, in the great testament of the prophets, the Passover and the Feast of Unleavened Bread are the most essential. They marked the miraculous deliverance from the angel of death who passed over those houses which were marked with the blood of the lamb, and they marked the release from bondage to Pharaoh that immediately followed. That was the beginning of Israel as a nation. In the Passover, the children of Israel, miraculously preserved and set free, became a people by the direct intervention of the God Who Is and the blood of the Lamb.

The Passover and the Feast of Unleavened Bread were kept in all the following years. God's people marked those great and defining historical events and gifts. But that which they marked was in itself only a mark of something else. They were buds awaiting the light of the incarnation to shine in the darkness, warm the soil, and bring life

---

† This image and phrasing is paraphrased and expanded from Alfred Edersheim, *The Temple, Its Ministry and Services as They Were at the Time of Jesus Christ.* (Bellingham, WA: Logos Research Systems, Inc., 2003). 209.

to light. The Passover and all the history of Israel opened as a flower at the nativity of our Lord. The angels sang and peace was declared. The earth bloomed in joy, but that bloom was still not the end. That from Mary's virgin womb matured. He was the loveliest fruit: the Lord Himself, in the flesh. And He ripened, became sweet and good for food for us upon the tree of life in the desolate garden of white-washed tombs, in the place of the skull, outside the City of Peace. There, strung up, hanging like that which once tempted Eve, now tempting Satan, is the fruit of God's love and the fulfillment of Israel's history and rites: our hope and salvation.

It is because the Passover was the most essential and central of Old Testament events that our Lord lays down His life in the midst of its remembrance. He goes as a lamb to the slaughter, silent, but not without knowledge. He lays down His life as a sacrifice, of His own accord, and He chooses the time. He is the Lamb whose blood shields us from the angel of death and delivers us from the slavery of Pharaoh. He is both the new Adam and the true Israel, and He is the One Who Is.

And if that simple, undeniable truth causes Caiaphas to rend his garments in mock piety, let it cause us to rend our hearts in humility and repentance. For the God Who Is and always has been, who set the continents into their place, carved out the oceans by His hand, and carries the sky upon His shoulders, has joined our cause, been born of the virgin, been sacrificed on the cross. He has become one of us, flesh of our flesh and bone of our bones. Our God is a man, come to be a sacrifice, a lamb, worthy of our sins, a wholly, holy substitute. The life His veins carried through this dying world is poured out upon the earth and down our throats to cleanse our broken hearts. Indeed, we ought then to rend our hearts and repent, that there be room for Him and His holy blood.

For this He was born, and for this He died: to have the body and blood that would be offered on our behalf, to give us that body and that blood as food and drink, sweet and satisfying to sinners desperately in need of forgiving food. On that holy night in which He was betrayed, on the very eve of His crucifixion and sacrifice, while yet in His humility, He gave His body and His blood *to us* which He would give on the next day *for us*. For this He was born, and for this He died.

He, His precious body and His holy blood, is the fruit of God's love, the culmination of history and the continuance of God's own nation. It was only a bud in Egypt, only a type in the lambs, bulls, and goats, only a promise yet to be fulfilled in the prophetic word. It flowered when the Lord preached on the mountainside. It flowered when He healed the sick and turned water into wine. But now it is mature. Now it is ripe. It has come to what it was intended for all along, to what was prophesied against the devil in the garden: It is the very means and substance of our reconciliation with the Father. We have a new tree, a new fruit, and a new way back to God. Thus are we, by grace, back where we belong.

The woman has a Seed. That Seed has grown and is fruit. That fruit restores us to the garden's fellowship and beyond. It undoes death and removes the curse. Here, in His Holy Supper, the Lord gives Himself to us, to eat and to drink, for the forgiveness of sins. This is what it is to be a Christian, not simply to be spared death but to have fellowship with God and to be sundered forever from the devil.

The fruit of the tree is on the paten and in the chalice. The angel of death passes over. He has no claim upon us. We belong to God. We bear His watery name. We eat at His table. We are His people and more. We are not merely guests, sojourners in His house for but an hour, but we are members of the royal family raised up from stones. We are not Gentile dogs hoping for crumbs, worshiping what we do not know. We, by grace, are the Lord's own beloved and immaculate bride. We belong to God. We are baptized. We eat at His table. We are gathered under the protecting shadow of the cross.

This is the Church of the New Testament. Christ Himself is her mediator. Like the Church of the Old Testament, it is a testament of blood. Christ, our Passover, has been sacrificed for us. His body and blood have been rent asunder in death and joined again in the resurrection. Let us celebrate the feast not with the old leaven but with the unleavened bread of sincerity and truth, with faith, hope, and love. For it is not merely the beauty of bud or flower that brings us joy tonight, but the full fruit of His love. And it is not merely our houses that are marked with the blood of the Lamb, but our very hearts and souls.

In ✠ Jesus' name. Amen.

Good Friday

Hosea 6:1-6
Exodus 12:1-11
St. John 18:1-19:42
Isaiah 53

In the name of the Father and of the ✠ Son and of the Holy Spirit. Amen.

Jesus is not described in the Gospels as "happy." As Isaiah foretold, He was a man of sorrows.

We are twice told, however, once by Luke and once by John, that Jesus rejoiced. Luke reports that "Jesus rejoiced in spirit, and said, 'I thank thee, O Father, Lord of heaven and earth, that thou hast hid these things from the wise and prudent, and hast revealed them unto babes'" (Luke 10:21 KJV).

This doesn't seem a particularly happy thing, that the Father has hidden Himself from the wise and prudent. But it causes Jesus to rejoice.

John tells us that Jesus said to His disciples, "Lazarus is dead. And I rejoice that I was not there, to the intent ye may believe" (John 11:14-15 translated from Greek). So next time you see a picture of Jesus laughing, imagine that He is telling the disciples, "Lazarus is dead."

Jesus rejoiced. I don't doubt that He also laughed. But overall, Jesus wasn't a happy man. He was a man of sorrows.

The emotion that the Gospels most often ascribe to our Lord is not, however, sorrow in terms of feeling sorry for Himself and the pain He must endure, but rather compassion. Compassion is "com," meaning "with," plus "passion," as in the passion of our Lord. Passion means to desire so intensely that it causes suffering. Compassion means to suffer *with*. Compassion is what happens to us when our sister tells us at Thanksgiving that she has had an abortion. We can't eat. As we mourn for the child we never knew, food loses its flavor. We realize the violence done to our sister and the baby came from ignorance or fear, but that it can't be undone. That frustration and pain is the main sorrow of the man of sorrows.

This is the nearly constant reaction of our Lord during the time of His humiliation. He looks about this fallen world and loses His appetite. He sees unnecessary sadness and pain everywhere, and it hurts Him to see others so unnecessarily sad. He sees the futility and stupidity of pride, greed, and lust. He watches us make bad decision after bad decision, out of ignorance or fear. He watches us hurt ourselves and those who love us, like girls going to an abortion clinic, thinking we will solve an inconvenient problem by a quick act of violence, when all we really do is strap ourselves to a lifetime of mourning and regret and place our bodies and souls in real danger.

Our Lord's other high-frequency emotion in the Gospels is anger. Sin makes God mad, mad enough to destroy the whole world in a flood, mad enough to bring the waves down on Pharaoh's head and turn Lot's wife into a pillar of salt, mad enough to make things so bad that the people would think barrenness was a blessing and beg the hills to fall upon them.

Good Friday is about God's wrath, like it or not. God's wrath is revealed as He casts it upon His Son on our behalf. Not just on Good Friday but throughout our Lord's ministry, we see His frustration, sadness, and anger over and at sin. He has no sympathy for the demons. And remember the fig tree He cursed. Remember the violence He inflicted upon the money changers. Remember how He called St. Peter "Satan." The lion of Judah, meek and mild, goes as a lamb to the slaughter without complaint, but He is no pussycat. He is the stronger man, and He is angry.

Then there is love. "Jesus loves me, this I know." Indeed. There may be no more profound statement in all the world. But that love is not what we usually think. That love is not Jesus sitting in heaven thinking happy thoughts about us. That love is sorrow, pain, and death.

Our problem is that we tend to think that ideal love is romantic love. Not every culture has thought in this way. Aristotle thought the highest form of love was friendship. But our modern-day movies about friendship, like *Homeward Bound* or *Toy Story*, are mainly for children. That is because our ideal love is something more like *The Titanic* or *Gone with the Wind* where love is magic and out of control. It can't be explained and it should never be suppressed. We can't help loving whom we love and can't be held accountable for crimes if they are meant to serve that ideal. "All you need is love," pined the Beatles, and we sang along as though we did not need clothing and shoes, food and drink, house and home, etc.

Our common view of love is even more selfish than it sounds. What we think of as love is really the contentment, peace, or happiness that others cause us to feel inside ourselves. What we are looking for in love is a soulmate who completes us, satisfies us, with whom we connect, so that when we spend time together the hours slip away in deep pleasure. Herein lies the cause of many a divorce because this kind of love is pure fantasy, and while it can be found for a short time in infatuation, it is not real and does not last.

Is there any more whiny and selfish complaint than "I just want to be happy?" Really? "Just" happy? Why not say you "just" want everything to be perfect. There is no such thing as "just" happy. Imagine our forefathers in the Battle of the Bulge or bound with chains in the bowels of a slave ship or facing surgery without anesthesia saying, "I just want to be happy." The statement is pure selfishness of the worst order. And if we haven't all said it, we've all thought it. Repent.

The problem with what we consider to be love is that it resides in the emotions of the lover. To some degree, love is how the lover feels about the beloved, but it doesn't take much of an examination to discover that what we really mean is how the beloved makes the lover feel, and that feeling is always good, positive, and enjoyable, or we would not call it love. You do not look at the man who raped your daughter and feel your heart grow full of joy and peace and contentment. Thus you do not say, "I love him. He is so sweet."

But this is how God loves us. His love for us does not make Him happy. Better than the Beatles is the rock band Nazareth: "Love Hurts." OK. Not really. That song is pure silliness, but the statement "love hurts" is closer to the truth. That is why mothers cry when their daughters marry. That is why we speak of the last days of our Lord's life as His passion.

John 3:16 is a key verse. The problem is that we mainly know that verse from the King James translation, and our English isn't very good. We hear the word "so" as emphasis. In fact, the Phillips paraphrase of the Bible, which seems to never paraphrase in the right way, reads, "God loved the world so much that He gave His only Son." Wrong. Let that be a lesson to you: Throw that piece of garbage out. No translation from the Greek would ever pull that. The KJV, unlike the Phillips, is not wrong; it is just that we can't hear it properly because we don't use the word "so" as that sort of an adverb very often. We do sometimes use the word "so" as it is used in John 3:16. We use it this way when we say, "Say it isn't so," or "Is that so?" We are not asking, "Say it isn't so much," but we are saying, "Say it isn't that way." The word the KJV translates as "so" means "thus," "in this way," or "in this manner."

In John 3:16, our Lord isn't writing a Hallmark card trying to declaim the great quantity or depth of God's love, like some cheesy country song. He is simply explaining to Nicodemus how it is that God loves the world: by giving His Son into death as a ransom for rebels who hated Him and killed Him and who chose Satan and Barabbas over Him. John 3:16 actually means, "For this is the way God loved the world: He gave His only-begotten Son so that whoever believes in Him should not be destroyed but have everlasting life." Remember that the sentence before verse 16 is Jesus saying that He must be lifted up from the earth. He is talking about His death. His death is how He loves the world, how He makes it His again.

Thus, St. John again: "Herein is love, not that we loved God, but that he loved us, and sent his Son to be the propitiation for our sins" (1 John 4:10 KJV). This is how the Lord loves rapists, abortionists, liars, back-sliders, and all the rest. This is how the Lord loves you. He gives Himself to death for them and for you. That love is sadness and anger, sorrow and pain.

Divine love, and human love that imitates it, is self-giving. It does not serve itself, but it serves the beloved. God's love for us does not fill Him with happy thoughts or make Him glad to see us. His love is service, action, death. God's love hurts Him, causes His heart to break and water and blood to pour out. We do not rightly understand love, in God or in ourselves, when we think of it as an emotion or a feeling. The emotions of Jesus in the Gospel are mainly sorrow and anger, not love, because love is not how He feels but what He does, who He is.

Yet, what the Gospels don't report in terms of emotion, the prophet Isaiah does: "Out of the anguish of his soul he shall see and be satisfied" (Isa. 53:11). The Gospels don't describe Jesus as happy, but Isaiah describes Him, in the end, as satisfied. That is something pretty close to happy. The Lord is satisfied because He has fulfilled His mission. It is finished, perfected, complete. He has loved and is loving His Father. He has defeated death.

Here is the great and wonderful surprise: You are the labor of His soul, the plunder of hell stolen away, the reward of the Father returned to its rightful place and beyond. You are His seed, the sons of God, the brothers of Jesus, the immaculate bride chosen in perfect grace, who are His generation and who also proclaim His generation. In this, in you, He is satisfied. By grace, you have believed our report and rejoiced in it. You are God's own beloved, whose iniquity is removed, whose sin is gone, whose shame is no more. And Jesus, King of the Jews, lifted up from the earth, has drawn you to Himself and is your Lord.

That is why we celebrate and rejoice in the sorrows of the man of sorrows. It is a good day. I prefer the Latin title *Tre Ore*, but the English is better than the German *Karfreitag*, which means funeral day or mourning day. Best said, today is Holy Friday. It is the day the Lord has made; let us rejoice and be glad in it. It is the day that belongs to Him, by which He sanctifies all men and by which He has recreated the world, upon which He finished creation. Certainly there is some truth in the title *Karfreitag*, but the emphasis is a bit off. We mourn for our sins, to be sure, but we also rejoice in the love of God revealed and showered upon us in the death of His Son. Yes, this is the way God has loved us: He has given Himself to us in death in order to give Himself, His crucified and risen body and blood, to us in the Holy Communion. If He had not died, there could be no testament. If His blood had not poured forth, it could not fill our chalice. And there is no remission apart from blood. When the faithful went to the tabernacle or the temple, they did so for blood, that their sins might be forgiven. So also we come to church. We come for blood, that our sins might be forgiven. God loves us in this way: He pours His blood onto our hearts through our mouths that we might be circumcised where it counts, that we might offer sacrifices not of blood, for that is offered to us, but that we might offer sacrifices of praise.

Here is God's love: He gives His Son. Good Friday is not bad or sad Friday. It is good Friday, for it is the day that the Lord restored the original goodness to His creation, and it is most certainly good for us. Good Friday is not a bad title, even as *Karfreitag* isn't either. Still, Holy Friday seems best to me, most inclusive of all the themes, for this is God's day above all other days, set apart for Him, the day of His victory, when the devil was put down at last, the day of His love, and the day that makes us His holy people as He Himself is holy.

We should love and embrace today, even as a bride embraces and loves her wedding day, for that is precisely what it is. And soon cometh the consummation, the departure of sadness, not when the stone is rolled away and Jesus is missing, but when Jesus enters into us in His risen body and blood and takes us for Himself, in the breaking of the bread. For know this above all, dear sad sinners: Jesus, who loves you, is risen and lives and is satisfied in you, that you are His.

In ✠ Jesus' name. Amen.

Easter Vigil

St. Matthew 28:1-7

In the name of the Father and of the ✠ Son and of the Holy Spirit. Amen.

B ehold, there was a great earthquake, for an angel of the Lord descended from heaven and came and rolled back the stone and sat on it."

The ESV obfuscates the causality of this earthquake; that is, as read from the ESV it may not be immediately clear what causes this earthquake, and I would have you know the cause. The angel is the cause. He does it. The word here translated "for" means "because," as in, "I did it for a good reason." The earth quaked for an angel of the Lord descended. He caused it. But this earthquake was only a show. It did not shake the stone loose. It is after the quake that the angel rolls the stone away. Then he sits on it.

I would like to know this angel's name. I like him. This angel is a bit of a showman and a jokester, but certainly, above all, he is a high church angel. His vestments are like lightning and white as snow. He is a showy, ostentatious, dramatic angel, unfit for low, cerebral celebrations of the strictly Protestant kind, but quite fitting for Easter in a catholic-minded place.

I think I know the answers, but I want to ask him, "Why the quake? Why the showy clothes? Why must you live out the songs that you wrote?"

My favorite part is when he sits on the stone. He is not tired. He, while looking like lightning, with clothing as white as snow, having just shook the ground for no good reason except to be a spectacle, now sits on the stone. He sits there to mock it. It is a puny stone, incapable of keeping Jesus in the grave, so he sits on it, as though to show both how insignificant it is and to keep it in its place.

And then look at how he ignores the temple guards. They are afraid. They tremble like the ground. But he ignores them. That is the force of the adversative conjunction which you non-English majors know as the word "but." "But" introduces a contrast dependent upon that which precedes it. "But the angel said to the women, 'Do not be afraid.'"

Who knew they were afraid? St. Matthew doesn't say the women were afraid. He says the guards were afraid. The guards were afraid, BUT the angel doesn't say anything to them. Instead, he says to the women, "Do not be afraid." The guards, it seems, should be afraid, and they should be glad he doesn't sit on them.

"Those who sow in tears shall reap with shouts of joy," sings the Psalmist (Ps. 126:5). But first he sings this:

> When the Lord restored the fortunes of Zion,
>   we were like those who dream.
> Then our mouth was filled with laughter,
>   and our tongue with shouts of joy;
> then they said among the [Gentiles],
>   "The Lord has done great things for them."
> The Lord has done great things for us;
>   we are glad. (Ps. 126:1-3)

Our sowing is complete. Jesus lives. Let us reap in joy, our mouths filled with laughter, as the angel sits upon that stupid, weak, and lying stone.

This Jesus, who was crucified, who went as weak as a kitten to the cross, has sapped the devil of all his strength. The trickster has been tricked. He ate the fruit that hung from the tree on Calvary, tempted and beguiled like Eve in the garden. He ate and now his belly bursts. His jaws are seared shut. He can take no more. He is done, finished, over. He has no accusations left. He hurled every last one of them at the Christ, and the Christ has answered for all of them, and there are none left for us or for anyone. Jesus died to take them away.

Did Satan then think that a rock or a guard could keep Jesus dead? The angels laugh at such a thought. Can a thimble hold the ocean? Can a dolphin swim to the moon? They hold Satan in derision. God is good. He gets His way. He won't be stolen from. He takes back what is His. He takes Eve, Gomer, us back out of slavery and prostitution and error. He has bought and paid for us and the devil has no claim. He got what he thought he wanted. He took a bite out of God. He bruised His heel. He spent all the fury of hell on Him and killed Him, put Him to death. But Jesus has crushed his head. The devil has nothing left. He cannot speak. He cannot lie anymore. Jesus died, but Jesus lives.

The angel sits on the stone, looking like lightning, clothes as white as snow, laughing at the devil. The grave is open. It won't hold Jesus. It won't hold your loved ones who have departed with the sign of faith. It won't hold you. Those who sow in tears, reap with joy.

Yes, I would like to know this angel's name. One day, God be praised, one day I will.

In ✠ Jesus' name. Amen.

EASTER

Job 19:23-27
1 Corinthians 5:6-8
St. Mark 16:1-20

In the name of the Father and of the ☩ Son and of the Holy Spirit. Amen.

O grave, where is your victory?

You swallowed up the Son of God, the Creator into creation. You took His lifeless body into your jaws. You captured God in the flesh. You brought the Creator so low that you stopped His breath, broke His heart, cut Him off from the light and the land of the living. You exacted a terrible price, the price of all the sins of all men, of the Law's full stricture, upon the sinless and perfect Son of God.

Is that your victory?

No. It is not. For the angel has rolled away the stone and showed the world that the Lord has escaped, that your strength has departed, that you could not hold Him, nor could the guards guard Him. It was as though they were dead. It is as though you are dead while Jesus lives again, out of the grave, back from the dead, raised alive and in the land of the living.

Where is your victory, O grave? Show me. Where is your sting? What has happened to your power? Have you so soon forgotten how you made us cower? Don't you claim to be the common lot of man, that we must all toil in this thorny place and then submit to you, our true master? Aren't you the ruler of the battlefield and cancer ward, the constant threat against young mothers, reminding us in every skinned knee, every mosquito bite, and every time we fall asleep, that you are the master and will take us when you want, even as you will and do take those we love? Don't you claim that you make our bodies fail, grow weak and old and contract disease, that you make this living death a pure misery of pain, dying, and loneliness, while you strive at all times to take away our dignity?

But we laugh with derision. We mock you. You, O grave, are dead, empty, and have lost all claim on us. Jesus lives. You have no victory, no sting. Jesus Christ is risen out of you and back to us. He has come out as a king to meet His people, as the general back from war, as the father racing toward us—His prodigal sons, prodigal no more—eager to take us back into the fold. The Lord has burst your walls from within, like new wine in an old wine skin. And now you, who could not hold Him, cannot hold us. On the last day, the dead will rise; everyone out of the grave, alive, will spring forth and face the rising Sun. No one, no, not one, will stay in the grave. You have lost.

They will be divided, to be sure. There is yet a distinction to be made between the goats and the sheep, the chaff and the wheat, the unbelievers and the believers, even as there is between God and Satan, life and death. For this living, risen God is not like you. He claims no dominion by power, even though power is rightly His. He will not force Himself. He will not steal. He does not demand. Those who do not want Him, who choose to remain in hell, to turn back to the grave, to persist in impenitence and make for themselves their own way, by their own laws, with their own mirror-image god—a god who just wants them to be "happy" and understands and rejects those old, moralistic attitudes of the Hebrews—then they can have what they want: They can go to hell. They will be raised only to be returned, to go with what is just, with what is theirs, with what they earned.

But to everyone who believes in Jesus Christ, the good and the bad, those who kept the fast and those who forgot or were lazy or who just did not care; to everyone who believes in Jesus Christ, whether honored or despised by men, whether rich or poor, whether full of virtue or scandal; to everyone who believes in Jesus Christ, eternal life and a place in the kingdom will be given—for free, as new wine in a new skin. They will come out of the grave in their bodies. The Lord will bestow upon them that which they did not earn and do not deserve, but which has been won for them by the sacrificial death of Jesus Christ, by His perfect life, by His immaculate grace. Strangely, the last will be first, the sinners will be saints. They will go with their God, with Jesus, into heaven to enjoy there the reunion of the ages.

But you, O grave, you will not get any of them, not even the goats. For you are undone and have no victory. Your wages have been paid. You are done, finished, perfected, and complete, once and for all. There is no more to ask, no more to pay. Your accusations against us have all been stripped away, nailed to a cross with the pledge, "King of the Jews." And by grace, we are Jews, sons of Abraham, circumcised in the heart, who live by faith and are reckoned righteous by grace, who share in the hope and expectation of Abraham, whose king is not you, but is Jesus Christ crucified and risen.

Now, all men have been reconciled to the Father in the death of Jesus Christ. No one who believes in Him, even if he sleep, will ever die. Jesus has risen for our justification. He has declared us righteous and holy and welcomes us to Himself in the Holy Communion. You can scowl, threaten, and attack, but you have lost. You are defeated. You have come to an end. Jesus lives!

So we bury our dead, O grave, only to mock you, not because they are dead, but because they live, because they are with Jesus, and their bodies sleep while they wait for the resurrection to come. We bury our dead because they have been sanctified and sealed for the resurrection through the risen body and blood of Jesus poured out on them in the Holy Communion. They go into you only that they might follow Jesus out of you and defeat you.

You think that is victory? It is utter defeat. But you get no pity, bitter tyrant, from us, for Jesus lives. He is our king.

So I ask again: Where, O grave, where is your victory? Where is your sting? They are gone. Jesus lives. And Jesus, alive out of the grave, is here for us—living, risen, in His holy body and His precious blood, the seal of the new life, the forgiveness of sins, the fellowship of the Holy Spirit, given to us to eat and to drink that we would never die and never suffer your lying tyranny.

Alleluia. Alleluia. Jesus lives.

Christ is risen . . .(He is risen indeed.)
Christ is risen . . .(He is risen indeed.)
Christ is risen . . .(He is risen indeed.)

In ✠ *Jesus' name. Amen.*

Easter Monday

Exodus 15:1-8
Acts 10:34-43
St. Luke 24:13-35

In the name of the Father and of the ✠ Son and of the Holy Spirit. Amen.

They had thought Him the One. They had thought He would save them, that He would redeem Israel. And now, they thought Him dead. The third day had come. The women had announced strange things. But they were troubled, afraid to believe. They didn't want to get their hopes up again.

And how does our Lord respond to their hedging hope, their carefully pessimistic belief? What does He say to their defense mechanisms that make them slow of heart to believe? He takes them through the Scriptures. Their hearts burn within them. Smoldering faith is rekindled in love, both by a rebuke—"O foolish ones, and slow of heart to believe," which is also a call to repentance—and by the uncovering of the promise. The prophets reveal to them who the Messiah is and what His office is. Our Lord uses the Scriptures to show the unchanging description of the suffering sacrifice of the Messiah to make men free and alive. This is not a new idea, a change of plan. Then He takes the bread, gives thanks, blesses it, and gives it to them. Their eyes are opened. They recognize the One crucified and raised, the One who has made atonement for them, the One who has loved them to the end and who feeds them with Himself in the bread, the One foretold and promised in Holy Writ. He disappears from the sight of their eyes. They know Him now by faith, faith that is born and lives in Word and in Sacrament.

It is the same for us. Do not be afraid to believe in the resurrection and all that implies for this dying life in which we still suffer. Be confident that God loves you, that He hears your prayers and answers them.

Find comfort in the sure and certain Word of God, in the presence of the risen Savior in bread and wine. For He who gave His life for you on the cross gives His life to you, here and now, in His body and blood. These are the blessings, the forgiveness, the joy He pours out upon His children—then, and now, and forever.

He is risen!

In ✚ *Jesus' name. Amen.*

Easter Tuesday

Daniel 3:8-28
Acts 13:26-33
St. Luke 24:36-48

In the name of the Father and of the ✠ Son and of the Holy Spirit. Amen.

An empty tomb is not enough.

An empty tomb could mean the disciples managed to steal the body or that Jesus was received up into heaven like Elijah, which is to say, an empty tomb could simply mean that the Lord hadn't really died; it had only seemed as though He died. Worse than that, though, an empty tomb could be a myth, a metaphor to say that Jesus rises when the hearts of His people come alive with faith. Rubbish.

What the eyewitness accounts provide is proof of the bodily resurrection of Jesus Christ. He shows the apostles His scars in order to show that He really did die, that He is the crucified One. He was slain as a substitute, in our place, so that the angel of death, having been sated in Him, would have no hunger for us and would pass over. He laid down His life as a ransom. He died to satisfy the Law's demands, to empty hell of its wrath and fury. He died. He has the scars to show it. But He has come through death. He is alive in His body.

That is why He eats with them and they handle Him. The point is that He died and He rose, but He is not a ghost or an angel. He is still a man. They, and we, have an advocate with the Father, a high priest who has endured all our temptations and overcome them. He paves the way into heaven, not for angels or saints but for men—and sinful men at that—for He who knew no sin became sin. Thus the very corpse, the very body, born of Mary, nailed to the cross, pierced by the centurion, dead and laid into the tomb, has been renewed and reborn. Our God is still a man, still one of us. He died, but He is alive, and heaven is open to sinful men.

The disciples believed, but they were worried, uncertain. Then He ate with them. And even as hearts in Emmaus were opened in the breaking of the bread, when the Lord was removed from their physical sight, so also there in Jerusalem: Hearts were opened. The apostles ate meat and broiled fish with God in the flesh, back from the dead, and their hearts were full of joy, faith, and peace.

It is not so different for you. Jesus is not apprehended by your eyes, but by faith. Not by gazing into an empty hole in the ground, but in the breaking of the bread under a visual reminder of the sacrifice. It is no accident that the Lord's Supper is consecrated on an altar under a crucifix. Here you eat with God. He gives you His body risen out of death. You handle Him. It is not a corpse. It is not a bloody piece of flesh, grilled medium-rare. It is the living, risen, glorified body, true man and true God, which God joins to bread to be your food, to satisfy your soul, to forgive your sins, and to encourage and strengthen your faith.

The empty tomb is not enough. What you need is the risen body of Jesus the crucified. And it is the risen body of Jesus the crucified that the Lord provides.†

In ✠ Jesus' name. Amen.

---

† Reworked from the Rev. Dr. Burnell Eckardt, http://gottesblog.blogspot.com/2008/03/empty-tomb-is-not-enough.html

The First Sunday after Easter— Quasimodogeniti

Ezekiel 37:1-14
1 John 5:4-10
St. John 20:19-31

In the name of the Father and of the ✠ Son and of the Holy Spirit. Amen.

We are bound to praise God for the goodness of this creation, for the joys of this earthly life, for rocks and trees and flowers and streams and chocolate and jelly beans.

So also we are bound to praise God for the gift of His Son upon the cross, for His being lifted up from the earth to finish death's reign of terror, hell's constant threats and sting, and Satan's accusations. He is the Paschal Lamb who was offered on our behalf, whose blood is smeared upon our tongues, that the angel of death passes over while we are safe and secure in the arms of our Father.

But chiefly—chiefly—are we bound to praise God for the glorious resurrection of Jesus Christ from the dead. In His dying, He has destroyed death. By His rising, He has restored us to everlasting life.

It is finished, perfected, and complete on the cross. The Father's wrath has been satiated in the death of the Son. He is no longer forsaken. Hell has had its fill. Death spits Him out like the whale spitting Jonah out upon the dry ground. Hell is repulsed from Him as the Red Sea withdrew from the children of Israel and allowed them to pass by on dry ground.

Is He not a weed, a shoot that has shot up from dry ground? And yet, He is not dead, nor parched. He is risen. He lives, and from His side come His lifeblood and water for the church, born out of death, born from above, born alive.

And thus are we bound chiefly to praise Him for His resurrection. As glorious as His death is, His life is more glorious. We preach Christ crucified. And yet the Church's main proclamation remains, "He is risen."

We see this in St. Thomas. The disciples had been warned about the resurrection. Even if the emphasis of the prophets and the Law was mainly on the sacrificial death of the Messiah, the Lord Himself had prophesied clearly that He would rise and when. But on top of this, by Easter evening they had had the reports of the women. They had been told that the grave had been opened and was empty except for angels announcing that it was as Jesus had said and that He is risen. Peter and John confirmed it. Then there were the two on their way to Emmaus, one of whom was probably St. Peter himself. And there was Mary Magdalene. So the two disciples on the road to Emmaus and Mary make at least three who had seen more than an empty tomb and angels. They had seen the risen Lord. All this had been reported in detail to the ten gathered in the upper room on Easter evening. But still they did not believe. Still, they were afraid.

Is it difficult to imagine why? Not if we are honest about our own sinful flesh and the power it has over us. It might be unreasonable, but certainly for us—who sin so frequently and grievously, who find a thousand ways to excuse ourselves, and who fear almost everything that walks this earth and even the things of our imaginations more than we fear the Lord—it should not be unimaginable. Repent. When it comes to obstinacy, unbelief, prejudice, and pride, the disciples have nothing on us.

But the Lord came to them despite their unbelief and fear, or maybe because of it. He stood in their midst. Locked doors and sealed stones do not keep His body out. He comes to them in the flesh, and He bestows His peaceful spirit upon them with a word.

Neither does His ascension to the Father's right hand keep Him from being bodily in the midst of His people this day and every Lord's day.

Yet a week later, with Thomas in place, the disciples' failure is much the same. We call these besetting sins, or pet sins, or just plain habits of sin. Again, it is fear of the Jews that causes them to lock the doors. The Holy Spirit has been bestowed upon them, already a week ago. The Lord has instituted and established the apostolic ministry. They have their marching orders. How, then, can they still be so unsure and afraid? Because they still abide in this fallen flesh, because the Holy Absolution, for the time being, removes guilt but not memory, consequences, or temptation.

It is the common lot of Christians still fighting in the church militant. Sins forgiven don't just go away. And those poor disciples, like unto us, must contend not only against hell and death but also against themselves, and our selves are the worst enemy of all.

The cure for this is the Word and the body of Jesus. They suffer from besetting sins. The Lord responds with besetting grace, abiding grace, a constant and ready application of His Word and body. The words here are "Peace be unto you," which is shorthand for the whole counsel of God and His mercy. The body is the body crucified, marked by those hateful nails that held Him in place. But the body crucified is alive, raised up again, joined back to His soul. That the Lord is risen is meaningless if He had not really been killed. If He had not been sacrificed on the cross, we would still be in our sins, even as we would still be in them if He were not raised.

Thus, Thomas is invited to see if those marks are real, that is, if this is really Jesus who really died as a sacrifice and is really back from the dead and—and—pay attention sinners!—to see if God has changed. For the perfected bodies of the saints bear no scars, but the risen Lord bears these. Thomas is not directed to look to the Lord's back marked by the Roman scourge or to His brow to see if there are marks from the thorns. He is pointed to the hands and side, to see what the cross has done to God in the flesh.

Has the cross changed God? Indeed. Yes! It has. It left marks.

Don't you throw your attributes and scholasticism at me. To say that God does not change is to try and imagine God from His own perspective instead of ours and that of Holy Writ. The Old Testament reports that God repents, that is to say, God turns, God changes His mind. So He has. He has changed His mind about us on the basis of His Son's holy death. His anger has been appeased. His wrath has been satisfied. We are not His enemies or rebels against Him. He is risen, come back alive from what we did to Him, but He seeks no revenge. We might expect Him to be angry at the disciples for their failures at the cross and their failures at the tomb, but He isn't. The blood that stains His garments is His own. He comes bearing peace and an invitation to fellowship.

Notice this: He submits to Thomas' ridiculous demands in perfect and steadfast mercy. From our perspective, which is the only one we can really know, as recorded in the Scriptures, we see and receive a change in God. He changes from wrath to mercy.

Yet this is none other than the God of Moses and Sinai. What was foreshown in shadowy form there is made clear in the incarnation. Jesus the Messiah is the mercy seat. He stands between us and the broken Law. He is the Lord who is eternal and without beginning, but He now has a beginning in the Virgin Mary and is created. He is changed in the cross and crucifixion, but we would not know it if He was not risen. He has done that which never will be done again. And now the ransom is paid, and He has instituted a new covenant in His blood. Wonder of wonders, He gives us His blood to drink, His body to eat! That which ought never to be done, because the life is in the blood, is now done, is given, and thereby God gives His life to us. The flow of the temple's blood has come to an end as Jesus' blood flows down our throats and upon our hearts. The temple is finished. The Law is finished. Death and hell and Satan and demons and disease are finished. For He is risen.

Thus are we chiefly bound to praise Him for His glorious resurrection from the dead. He is in our midst, according to His promise, in His risen, living, physical body, speaking peace, forgiving sins, feeding saints, and encouraging faith. No locked doors, no synodical bureaucrat, no bully, no fallen flesh will keep Him out.

Thanks be to God, Jesus lives.

In ✠ Jesus' name. Amen.

THE SECOND SUNDAY AFTER EASTER—
MISERICORDIAS DOMINI

Ezekiel 34:11-16
1 Peter 2:21-25
St. John 10:11-18

In the name of the Father and of the ✠ Son and of the Holy Spirit. Amen.

I don't know why, I suppose it is defensiveness, but whatever the reason, it seems as though single mothers are constantly telling me that the father, or fathers, of their children are "good dads," when, in fact, I know that they are dirtbags. What the mothers mean is that the fathers enjoy playing with their children when it is convenient. They are good, for a few moments at least, at making their children giggle. They enjoy the cuteness of their kids. They mainly like their children, even if they find them largely inconvenient and easy to forget.

These dads tend to be terrible, if not completely worthless, providers. They rarely, if ever, pay for their children's food. They don't change diapers or help around the house. They certainly don't teach their children the Ten Commandments or the Lord's Prayer. But since they enjoy their children and their children desperately enjoy the fleeting moments of their attention, the moms judge them to be "good dads," and I suppose, depending on your definition of "good," maybe they are. If nothing else, they seem to be good at impregnating girls they have no intention of marrying.

That little tirade is meant to introduce the difficulty we have in understanding our Lord's proclamation that He is the Good Shepherd. Dictionary.com lists forty-one ways that "good" can be used as an adjective in English. Not all of them can be applied to the Good Shepherd. By my count, about twenty of them can be. But, of course, the Lord didn't say in English, "I am the Good Shepherd."

He probably spoke in Aramaic, though it is very possible that He spoke in Hebrew, and it is remotely possible that He spoke in Greek. In one sense it doesn't matter what language He spoke. The Holy Ghost has given it to us in Greek. And what the Holy Ghost gives is authoritative. So you may as well learn a Greek word today. The word here translated "good" is the word *kalos*. Jesus is the *kalos* Shepherd.

Those dirtbag dads might be good dads depending on what we mean by the word "good." But they would never be considered *kalos* dads. And that is the distinction we need to keep in mind. There is a romantic notion of the Good Shepherd that thinks of the Good Shepherd the way those single moms think of the dirtbags. It thinks that the goodness of the Shepherd abides in His affection for the sheep. So a good dad is a dad who likes the fun parts of being a dad, and a good shepherd is one who likes to pet and cuddle sheep for his own amusement. He is good at deriving pleasure from others.

Now, in fairness, that idea about God is not completely out of place in the New Testament. The Lord does, in fact, hold you in deep affection. He does love you as a father loves his children. He also loves you as a husband loves his wife. He loves you as a colleague and a comrade. His bond and love for you embraces all the ways humans love one another, but more purely, without self-interest or jealousy or fear.

So there is nothing wrong with thinking of Jesus as the kindly, gentle lover of sheep. Fine. But as correct as that sentiment might be, it just isn't what these passages are about. He isn't saying, "I am the gentle lover of sheep." He is saying, "I am the *kalos* Shepherd."

That means that He is saying that He is the right Shepherd, the fitting, uniquely qualified and best Shepherd for sinners. He is, in fact, the only Shepherd who can actually bear this title. David and his sons were only types, shadows of the gracious rule of the *kalos* Shepherd. So also, our pastors are but echoes of the true Shepherd. That is what *kalos* means. It means good, right, fitting. It means true, beautiful, and accurate. It means competent, good for you, and worthy of praise.

Our Lord's primary purpose in this proclamation is to deny the claims of all other shepherds. He denies the claim of the many shepherd gods and kings of the Greeks and other pagans and, at the same time, he denies the claim of the Pharisees, Priests, and Essenes. If you are a shepherd, whether you are King David or Pastor Jones, you must be an undershepherd, a shepherd who shepherds not his own sheep, but who is himself a sheep of the *kalos* Shepherd and whose office is to proclaim that *kalos* Shepherd as the receiver and savior of sinners.

The Lord can make this claim, that He is the *kalos* Shepherd, because He is good in the sense of morality. He is morally perfect, without sin. But His claim comes not from morality, but from faithful obedience and sacrifice. The Good Shepherd, the *kalos* Shepherd, is the true Shepherd because He gives His life for the flock. He overcomes the wolf by filling the wolf's mouth with His own body and thus saves the sheep from being lost. He is one with the Father, so His people, His sheep, bought with His own blood, become one with the Father: one flock, one Shepherd. He is King Messiah.

The great hope and expectation of the rabbis who taught before Christ was that the Messiah would unite all the Jews of Palestine, all the Jews of the *diaspora*, and all the Gentiles into one flock. They taught that King Messiah would destroy the temple and usher in a new age, a new law and covenant, and there would be no separation of Jew and Gentile. This, in large part, is why the rulers of the Jews fear Jesus. They weren't so afraid that He was a fraud. They were afraid that He was the Messiah, and they didn't want a Messiah; they didn't want the Gentiles or the end of the temple.

Our Lord, then, is claiming that by sacrifice, He, the *kalos* Shepherd, will reconcile sinners to the Father and make one flock. This is the character of the true and noble Shepherd, beautifully fit for His purpose, competent, good, worthy of praise—all that is confessed in the term *kalos*.

That is why I don't like much of the art work that this passage has inspired. It tends to concentrate too much on the idea of Jesus as gentle lover of sheep and pays too little attention to the key passage: "I lay down My life for the sheep." Again, the goodness of our Shepherd is not in His affection, but in His sacrifice. And if His affection is the cause of His sacrifice, then note this: It is not His affection for us, but His affection for His Father.

That is a tough lesson when you've been raised on the corn syrup theology of the gentle lover of the sheep, but it has its rewards. In the first place, it is Biblical. It comes out of our Lord's own description of His mission and His motives, and not from some mewling attempt to be winsome or nice. Secondly, it takes the focus off of us and places it where it belongs: on Him. He lays down His life. He takes it up again. His Father loves Him because of it. We are but the spoils of war, the plunder rendered to the Son by a grateful and affectionate Father. We are the sheep of a different fold, brought in without pedigree or works, spared from the hired hands.

We have heard His voice in His Word as given by the Spirit. We have heard Him call our names in Holy Baptism and wrap them in His own name. We have heard His promise and in Him we know also His Father. The charge He was given, to save us, He has fulfilled—whether we are "baby daddys," "prostitutes," "Gentiles," or "racists." He is good. He is *kalos*. And He is risen. He is risen indeed. Hallelujah!

In ✠ Jesus' name. Amen.

SOLEMN VESPERS OF MISERICORDIAS DOMINI

1 Peter 2:21-25

In the name of the Father and of the ✠ Son and of the Holy Spirit. Amen.

St. Paul famously proclaims, "We preach Christ crucified." St. Peter also reminds us that Christ bore our sins in His body. But it isn't just the apostles who are obsessed with the death that Jesus died; it is also the angel who announces the resurrection to the women at the tomb. He tells them, "Do not be frightened. You seek Jesus of Nazareth, who was crucified. He has risen."

His resurrection is not merely meaningless, but it is worthless if He has not died and died as a sacrifice for sins. The point of "He is risen" is always "He died."

That is what St. Thomas, in his doubt, wants proof of. They tell him that Jesus lives. He wants proof—the marks in His hands and feet and side—of His death. We might be tempted to think that was Thomas in his unbelief, and therefore lacking. But it was those very marks, the marks of our Lord's crucifixion, that convinced St. Thomas that Jesus was not just God and Lord, but his God and his Lord.

In the same way, in St. Luke's Gospel we read that our Lord's post-death appearance to the disciples causes them fear. They think He is a spirit. He says, "Why are you troubled, and why do doubts arise in your hearts? See my hands and my feet, that it is I myself. Touch me, and see. For a spirit does not have flesh and bones as you see that I have" (Luke 24:38-39).

If He is a spirit and has not a body, they should indeed be afraid. But He seeks to both convince and calm them with an appeal to His hands and His feet. We should note this. This is not the way that we would identify ourselves to some old acquaintance who has forgotten us.

We would say, "Look into my eyes," or "Remember the time that you and I did this or that." Most of us would have trouble identifying the hands of our wives, husbands, or children if that was all we had to look at. It is not the part we focus on or think of as holding the personality.

The Lord's hands and feet are marked in a unique way, of course, but that is not the point. The point is how He got them. He has prints, marks, left by the nails that fastened Him to the altar of the cross. More than being unique marks in the history of humanity, they are the marks of His office. They are proof that He died in obedience to His Father's charge as a sacrifice for Thomas and for all of us.

Some of you may remember the widespread graffiti of the 1970s that read, "Frodo lives." Few in this world would wish more than I that Frodo lives, but he doesn't. The graffiti, I think, was born from something broken in us that wanted Frodo to live more than we want Jesus to live. Frodo, or perhaps Aslan or some other fictional character, can seem more appealing, more real, than Jesus to our fallen flesh.

Repent. The fault lies not with Tolkien or Lewis or fantasy literature in general. The fault lies with us who are always looking for idols to replace God even when we don't know it. Not every golden calf has been fashioned out of gold. Idols are made out of all the substances of earth, including imagination, but most are made out of pride.

Despite our reluctance to have the crucified Lord, it is the crucified Lord that we need. Frodo can't save us. Jesus lives is only good news because Jesus died. Only God can save us and only then, according to His own will and Law, by His Law being fulfilled. The only way His Law can be fulfilled is for Him to fulfill it. We can't fulfill His Law. Even if we could, we could only do so for ourselves, or maybe we could substitute ourselves for one other person, but then we would be condemned. So He fulfills His own Law. He takes up our cause. He will not let the devil have us. He will not let the devil win. He becomes a human, bone of our bone, flesh of our flesh, a body and soul taken from the virgin womb of Mary in order to keep the Law. He commits no sin, and then He entrusts Himself to Him who judges justly.

And what is the just judgment of Him who did not sin? Guilty of our sins and accountable for all the Father's wrath, all of hell's fury, all the devil's lies and all the devil's truth. All of it is spent on Him as He is suspended from the earth, lifted up on the altar of the cross, removed from His Father and removed from creation. He gives Himself to the Father as a sacrifice. He is a ransom and a payment for our sins. He who knew no sin, became sin. He is judged and condemned, and Barabbas goes free. "He himself bore our sins in his body on the tree, that we might die to sin and live to righteousness. By his wounds you have been healed."

But then the payment is complete, finished, and there is no more to pay. There is nothing more to say, no accusations left in our ancient enemy, no more crimes or sins in all of the wide world. Then, and only then, He died. He loved us to the end. Then, when He was ready, when it was finished, then He died.

His body and His soul were separated. His body went to the ground to rest for one final Sabbath. His soul went to His Father.

And then—oh, yes!—then He rose. Early on the third day, His body and His soul came back together again. As a man, in His body, He passed through the stone they sealed to keep Him in, even as that night He would pass through, in His body, the door that was locked in fear to keep Him out.

The real surprise in Easter is not that He lives. We expect the living God to live. The surprise is that He died, was crucified to death, and that He is not angry and holds no grudge. There are a thousand reasons that the disciples should have been afraid. They failed, terribly, on Good Friday and throughout their lives. They were not brave. They were not loyal. They were not good, and they were not either believing or faithful. If God were to hold them to any standard, they would be destroyed.

But the One who died, whom they betrayed and failed, came to die. He came to be a sacrifice and was announced to shepherds in their fields as the source of peace. He comes in peace. He stands in their midst, in His body, and speaks peace upon them. He is not angry. He bears no grudge. The sacrifice is complete. The payment is full. God is pleased with them and desires their company at the banquet of His Son. Jesus, the crucified one, the only one who should not die, died. Thanks be to God, Jesus died. But He is not dead; Jesus lives. He died, to be sure, thanks be to God, He died, but He is not dead. He lives.

So, too, will all those who believe in Him.

In ✠ Jesus' name. Amen.

THE THIRD SUNDAY AFTER EASTER—
JUBILATE†

_____

† This was Confirmation Sunday at Redeemer.

Isaiah 40:25-31
1 Peter 2:11-20
St. John 16:16-22

In the name of the Father and of the ✠ Son and of the Holy Spirit. Amen.

Three times, prior to the crucifixion, the Lord warns His disciples that He will be taken from them by betrayal, injustice, and violence. Then, after being killed, He will rise again on the third day. Here, He warns them in a different way. They draw near to the time when they will see Him no more. Then, after a while, they will see Him again. He predicts the sorrow they will have at His death and the joy they will have at His resurrection. They will fail Him, but He will not fail them. They will be unfaithful and abandon Him, but He will return for them in perfect love and faithfulness, without anger, after He rises from the dead.

This is why the confirmands qualify their pledges with "by the grace of God." By grace, they intend to hear the Word of God and to receive the Lord's Supper faithfully. That is, they intend to come to church every single week to hear the preaching and for the Holy Communion. By grace, they intend to live free of sin, to keep God's Law. They would rather die than sin. By grace, they intend to continue steadfast in the confession they have made according to Luther's Small Catechism, and here, too, they would rather die than fall away from this confession. They have this intention by grace. They will fulfill this intention by grace or not at all. If and when they fail, they will repent and throw themselves again upon Christ's mercy because He will not fail them.

In light of the Lord's promises to the apostles and our own experience, thinking of what confirmands and apostles might need, we may ask ourselves, "Why, after the resurrection, does the risen Lord ascend to the Father instead of staying with the disciples here on earth?" For it might well seem as though Christ ought to have lived on earth with His disciples after the resurrection. We know that when they saw Him, as promised, that it confirmed their faith in the resurrection and in His love. It brought them comfort in their disturbed state. It banished fear. St. John says it with profound simplicity: They were glad when they saw the Lord.

So wouldn't they have been more assured, more consoled, and more glad if He had stayed with them here on earth? And not only they, but so also our tender confirmands, and we ourselves?

No. Because after the resurrection two things had to be manifested to the disciples: the truth of the resurrection and Christ's glory. The truth of the resurrection was proved by several appearances and demonstrations of bodily reality, mainly through touching and eating. But in order to manifest the glory of the risen Christ, the Lord had to ascend. After the sacrifice was complete and His humiliation ended, He did not live with them, or with us, as He had before.

Hence, in Luke 24 He says, "These are my words that I spoke to you while I was still with you" (v. 44). He said that to them while He was with them in His body. They touched Him. He ate and drank with them. He is not a spirit or a ghost. He is a man, body and soul, risen from the dead, alive. But even as He says that, while He is with them in His risen body, He is not with them anymore in His humility. There has been a change. The Father has accepted the sacrifice. The Son is vindicated. As a man, He now uses, fully, all the time, His divine rights and attributes. He is with them still in His body, but no longer as a mortal, no longer racing toward death.

Christ's frequent appearing in His body served to assure the disciples of the truth of the resurrection. But if He had continued in that presence, it might have confused them into thinking that there had been no real change, that He rose to the same life as He had lived before. So He departs, ascends, for their sakes, that they would know His glory and accept His new bodily presence in the breaking of the bread. By that new presence, established as the New Testament on the night when He was betrayed, He promises them comfort in another life. He didn't rise to the same life He had lived before, and He doesn't bestow upon us the same life we now live. He gives us, in the Holy Communion, life eternal. Thus, today's Gospel: "I will see you again, and your hearts will rejoice, and no one will take your joy from you."

That is the joy we are waiting for, eager and expecting. Jesus has given His life for ours yet now lives and is present among us in His body and blood, to bestow that new life and joy. Here is grace for confirmands to keep their vows: the bodily presence of the risen Christ, for you, in the Holy Communion. By grace they promised, by grace they confessed. May we all do the same, trusting in God's promises.

In ✠ Jesus' name. Amen.

THE FOURTH SUNDAY AFTER EASTER—CANTATE

Isaiah 12:1-6
James 1:16-21
St. John 16:5-14
Psalm 98

In the name of the Father and of the ✠ Son and of the Holy Spirit. Amen.

The Lord has done marvelous things. They are greater in number than the imprecise mathematics of men dare to count, more marvelous than our feeble minds might comprehend. He has called the galaxies to be, set the planets on their course, established the infinite depth of all black holes. But so, too, do Zeus and Mohammed's Allah (or at least according to those who imagined them) claim to be creators.

God breathed life into men. He created all the living. He taught the plants to grow. He carved the paths of rivers and built mountains. But so, too, do Zeus and Allah make these claims, and even the Great Spirit or the Architect in the sky.

And the devil says, "See. 'Gods' are all the same. Any name will do. Call him what you want. It does not matter to him or to me. We have more in common than not. Unity is the highest goal. We should all be nice."

But the devil always lies. Those things of creation are marvelous, but they are not gracious. And so, too, is morality good. Where the pagans agree with God concerning morality, thanks be to God. But like those things of creation, there is no grace in morality. Creation and morality are not so different from what a man might imagine would interest a god. Repent.

The God of Abraham in the flesh from Mary's womb is not imagined, nor is He like us. He has remembered His mercy. His right arm has gotten Him the victory. He submitted to defeat in humility to break death's teeth. He died and He rose again. He lives. Unlike Zeus or Allah or any imaginary god fired in men's fantasies by demonic impulse, our God died to pay for the sins of men who rejected Him. Our God died for us. That is the truth. He has sent the Comforter to comfort us with that truth, for that truth sets men free. His love is perfect and forgiving. It reconciles sinners to the Father. It gives us a song to sing, not of idle fancies but of history and of the future.

Though He was angry with us for our vile and selfish deeds, His wrath has been turned to the cross. It has been spent upon the Son. Our God sent His Son to die for us and to rise again! We could not have guessed what God would do to make us His, to buy us back again. We could not have expected or imagined such love. He has become our salvation, our strength, and our song. He has taken the sins of the world into His body. The accuser has been robbed of his accusations. Jesus died for us and crushed the liar's head. He let us kill Him rather than send us to hell where we belonged. He is not fair; rather, He is merciful. He is gracious and forgiving.

Death has no more claim upon us because He took our place. He died our death. It is finished. Death is now empty. There is nothing left. He rose up out of the grave, alive in His body on the third day, reunited with His soul, the victor over hell. The grave did not hold Him, and it cannot hold us. Like unto His glorious body, our bodies will be raised and perfected.

This is the most marvelous thing. It defines our God and gives us a song. Our Lord and the holy apostles call it the Gospel. It is the power of God unto salvation. It is the content of our song and also the cause of our singing.

Marvelous things! He has ascended to the right hand of His Father. He rules in the hearts of those who believe in Him in perfect grace.

They call Him Lord and King. Once He was so mocked, now is He so worshiped. INRI is not mockery in our mouths, but confession and praise: "Jesus of Nazareth, King of the Jews, our God and our Lord." And from the Father's side He has sent the Helper, that Holy Spirit who once hovered over the chaos and brought it into order. He is the Spirit of Truth. He teaches us to pray. He grunts out for us perfect prayers that words cannot express. He inspires the apostles and prophets to write His words. He glorifies the Son by taking what is the Son's as well as the Father's—perfection, righteousness, innocence, holiness—and declaring it all to be yours, and all for free. He delivers Jesus. And where there is Jesus, there is also life and salvation. And where there is life and salvation, there is singing.

We cannot help ourselves. It springs up from the depths of our souls. Our joy overflows. We are forgiven. We are loved. Our lives have purpose and meaning. The Spirit inspires us and puts His words, through David, upon our lips, and we sing the new song of redemption.

Marvelous things! He has intervened in the course of human affairs to bring about our salvation. He has driven a tent peg through Sisera's head and burned Ba'al's prophets. He has scared the Canaanites into killing one another with nothing more than Gideon's name and some torches. He has caused the wheels to come off of Pharaoh's chariots and the waters to come crashing in around his army. He struck the temple guards who watched the tomb. It is as though they were dead. They cannot speak or complain. They cannot hold Him there or keep us out. He broke the seal. He came through the door. He breathed upon those apostles to deliver His Holy Spirit and the keys to heaven. He has seen to all the details. He has missed nothing

Marvelous things! God has called you to be. He has given you a Mother who has birthed you in the Jordan's bloody waters, made you clean by grace. She has raised you in the fear of the Lord and taught you to pray. She has reminded you of your grandfather Abraham, your uncle Jacob, your distant kinsman Job. She brings you to the body and the blood for you to eat and to drink, to sustain you for your labor, and to seal your future. She is the Church, the handmaiden of the Lord, and she serves you as her own dear child. She is a holy, Christian Mother and as all her daughters do, she also prays for you. For behold, the prayers of a righteous man, be he male or female, avail much.

So sing unto the Lord a new song. For He has done marvelous things.

In ✠ Jesus' name. Amen.

The Fourth Sunday after Easter—
Rogate

Numbers 21:4-9
James 1:22-27
St. John 16:23-33

In the name of the Father and of the ✠ Son and of the Holy Spirit. Amen.

We can reduce the fads of pop-Christianity into two camps: those that want to make people behave and those that promise prosperity. The distinction between the two might be a bit artificial since the point of making people behave is usually to attain prosperity.

40 Days of Purpose is an example of a recent attempt to make people behave. So also did Promise Keepers and the WWJD bracelets want to make us better people. Perhaps the crassest gimmick for prosperity ever tried was a book entitled *The Prayer of Jabez*. It claimed that if you prayed this obscure passage in the Old Testament every day and night, you would be prosperous. Lots of people did. Jesus never did. Isn't that amazing? Imagine advocating that the way to trick God into being nice to you was to pray something that Jesus never prayed. And even before those things, there was Norman Vincent Peale's *The Power of Positive Thinking*.

In fairness, most of these fads hold a sliver of truth. Moral behavior does make for a much more satisfying life. It often brings a kind of prosperity. It is hard, for instance, to be prosperous in prison. Divorce is expensive. But so too can successful criminal lifestyles bring prosperity. Fidel Castro lives in luxury. So did Saddam Hussein. Prosperity doesn't prove morality. Having a purpose in life, defined by the name of God given in baptism, keeping your promises, and behaving like Jesus are all good and healthy things. It is also true that believing God is good and that He wants to bless you, coupled with morning and evening prayer, is a very good thing. God does want to bless you.

The problem with all of these fads is that they stand apart from the death and resurrection of Jesus Christ. They are gimmicks. They are all befuddled by our Lord's prophecy: "In the world you will have tribulation."

The model for Christian prayer is the garden of Gethsemane. Our Lord asked that the cup be removed, but it was not. Even as the Father would forsake the Son on the cross in order to be with us, so also He denied the Son's request in the garden in order to grant our requests. The Father's will is that all men turn and be saved, that all the world be reconciled to Him, that all creation be sanctified and returned to Him. The Father loves the Son in the Son's laying down of His life to fulfill His will and in His taking it up again. But what was finished on the cross has not yet been completed in time. Not all the elect are yet baptized.

Jesus Christ is the victor over the world. He has defeated the last enemy. He is alive out of the grave to bring us to His Father's side. Yet the tribulation continues while God delays the last judgment, and the angels restrain the destructive winds, in order to get all His children to safety.

That is not to say that it is wrong to pray for prosperity. You have been baptized into Christ. The fullest and most personal, revealed name of God—Father, Son, and Holy Spirit—has been placed upon you. You are clean and acceptable to God. You are forgiven. He makes Himself available to you through that name in prayer.

You always pray as a child to his father. Perhaps you come at times on bended knee, afraid of His wrath for your sins, or you address Him as "Almighty Creator" or even "Judge of the World." But even then you come because you have been washed in the blood of the Lamb and made clean, because you know that He loves the Son, and in the Son He loves you and has bestowed His Spirit upon you.

Solomon was no fool when he asked for wisdom, as though he just stumbled upon that idea. It took wisdom to ask for wisdom. So also you come to the Father in the Spirit through the Son, knowing what His promise is. It takes faith to ask for faith, forgiveness to ask for forgiveness. No one confesses his sins to God without expecting the gracious, living Lord to remove them. Baptism might have been a surprise, even as the resurrection was, to a degree, but the absolution is never a surprise because it is always and only faith that asks for it. Meditate sometime on the general confession we say at the beginning of the Divine Service. It is not the confession of a trembling, scared person. It is a confident request that expects grace. Even without the absolution—not that we would ever have it without the absolution, but even without it—our rite for the confession of sins is comforting.

Your prayers and your life in Christ are defined by the name of God which He has given you: Father. You pray with the boldness and confidence of dear children asking their dear father. What do children ask their fathers for? Food? A home? Safety? Maybe. Occasionally. But not mostly.

Mostly, children ask their fathers for frivolous things: for toys, for sweets, for attention. When children do ask for the needs of someone else, or for necessities of daily life, it is when something is terribly wrong and they are broken-hearted. Children will almost always ask their fathers to give the beggar at the bus stop some money or to heal the bird with the broken wing. But if things are going well, they don't ask for a house or for their father to be nice to their mother.

Here is the point: Praying for yourself and for prosperity is not wrong. It is natural. And it does not annoy your Father in heaven. Much of what you ask is frivolous. What else would you expect of children? He knows what you actually need. He provides it even when you don't ask. But do not underestimate the power of intercessory prayer. The earthly father at the bus stop may have hardened his heart. He has seen too many beggars drinking from brown paper bags. He fears the beggar will abuse any money he is given. But when the child asks, the father is moved and fulfills the child's request. This is not a perfect analogy because our Father in heaven is not cynical or selfish. But your prayers are effectual. They make a difference in the world. God acts because of them. Do not make light of it. God does more than change your heart through prayer: He also acts because of your prayer.

Thus He has called you to pray. By your prayers creation is spared, chaos is fought back, pollution is removed, the world is cleansed. Do not worry about making your prayers orthodox or asking for the right things. Just pray for what you want. You want to be thinner. You want the zit to go away before the date tonight. You want some ice cream, or you just want to not be bored. And in the same breath, you want a cure for cancer, an end to AIDS in Africa, peace in the Middle East. Fine. The world is polluted. Your heart is broken. Do not harden it. Open it to God. Make your petitions in the name of Jesus, in boldness and confidence, without fear.

On this side of glory you always pray from the garden of Gethsemane, never from heaven. Jesus has overcome the world, but you still abide in it. Rejoice and thank God for those times when He gives you the joys of this creation, like dinner with friends and feet washed by Jesus. But also submit to His goodness and will. You are, after all, but a child. You do not know what is best. You are not in control. You wait for His goodness to be revealed, trusting that He will bring you to Himself in heaven, that He forsook the Son to never, never forsake you.

The tomb is empty. You are joined to Him in the holy eating and drinking of His body and blood. You will also rise from the dead. This is the peace He bestows with His Holy Spirit. It passes all understanding. You need it now because you have not yet arrived. The day will come when you will ask Him for nothing. Now, you ask Him for everything. That is what beggars and children do.

That is the Christian view of and desire for prosperity. We'll take it when and where it comes, where God gives it, and we will not be ashamed to ask for it. But neither will we seek to manipulate Him into it. We will suffer and wait for His goodness to be revealed. His will is good. His will will be done.

Now to the other pop-Christianity fad: better behavior. We'll take that too. St. James exhorts us to be doers of the Word and not hearers only. But that behavior comes not by gimmicks and slogans or a by the resolute setting of human will; it comes in prayer. That is how God's Word is done, how you do God's Word: You pray. God's Word is first heard. It enters into you, then it comes out again. God's Word on your lips makes you a doer of God's Word. He speaks, and then you speak His Word back to Him.

That is not to make light of the moral law and of the things that something like Promise Keepers wants to uphold. We are not against it, in a sense, but that is more of a passive thing: not breaking God's Law, not cheating on your wife, not stealing and lying, and such. Those things are indeed dangerous to faith. But God's Word is done to us when we are convicted of our sins and then forgiven our trespasses, when the righteousness of Jesus Christ is proclaimed to be our own and we are welcomed by name into God's gracious presence. As those who hear God's Word first, we then do God's Word in prayer and praise and thanksgiving. The goal is not that we be good; the goal is that we be declared good in Christ and stay ever dependent upon Him.

God the Son, our Lord Jesus Christ, was never alone on earth—even in the desert, in Gethsemane, or on the holy cross. The Father was ever with Him in the Spirit. The angels never averted their eyes.

So also, you are never alone. You stand with baptized feet and hands before the Father in the Spirit through the Son. And as you stand, you pray, and your Father in heaven is pleased, so that whatever you ask Him, He gives. Thus your joy will be full.

In ✠ Jesus' name. Amen.

ASCENSION

2 Kings 2:5-15
Acts 1:1-11
St. Mark 16:14-20
St. Luke 24:44-53

In the name of the Father and of the ✠ Son and of the Holy Spirit. Amen.

The Lord gives the Law, the prophets, and the Psalms. More than that, He gives light to read them. He opens them. He bestows a mystery and a code more profound than that imagined by Dan Brown or Harold Camping. "All the Scriptures," He says, "concern Me."

What was the mind of Moses, the hope of Elijah, the sight of Isaiah? That the Christ, God's own Messiah, the One anointed as the Savior, should suffer and die and on the third day rise again from the dead, and that repentance and forgiveness of sins should be proclaimed in His name to all the Gentiles, beginning at Jerusalem.

The Gospel began, as it always does, with the preaching of repentance. John stood in the wild place and exposed the dark hearts of men by the Word of God, that they would turn from their sins and throw themselves upon God's mercy. Now the Gospel begun is complete. He has fulfilled the Gospel in His suffering. He has ended the Father's wrath, hell's demands, Satan's accusations, and the cry of justice against us. There is good news for men because Jesus died; because Jesus became sin and a curse, a worm and no man; because our sins have been pushed into Him, and He pushed off the edge into Gehenna in our place. It is finished. It is done. It is over, perfect, complete, and there is peace for the angels to announce to shepherds.

Now that the sacrifice long foretold is complete, the Christ solemnly and emphatically insists that repentance is the great fact of New Testament preaching. The Church is to "open their eyes, and to turn them from darkness to light, and from the power of Satan unto God" (Acts 26:18 KJV). And with this repentance, the forgiveness of sins in Christ is also ever to be preached. In this, the forgiveness of sins, men are made to see and hear and read the Holy Scriptures, to know God in the Christ as the fulfillment and purpose of all creation. Thus the Scriptures were opened to them and thus the Scriptures, by grace, are opened to us.

God's will is constant. Fallen men need a preaching of repentance, an exposure of our complicity and selfishness, a warning of impending death, and an invitation. You are not God. You do not make the rules. You have not behaved in ways honorable or just or good. You have looked the other way. You have cheated. You are a traitor to your own cause, in league with demons, a pervert, a deviant, a sycophant, a liar, a braggart, a hypocrite, a bureaucrat. Repent. Submit. Stop making excuses. Do not seek to have your sins justified but seek instead to have them forgiven, removed, and counted against Him, that His good works might be counted to you.

The Lord doesn't justify sins. He doesn't wink and nod. He doesn't understand or simply realize that to be human is to be a sinner. Because it isn't true. He is a human and He didn't sin. What He does is declare sinners to be just for His sake, as the beneficiaries of His sacrifice, substitute, and ransom.

God has sent His Christ for you. He is historical. He lived in the time of Pontius Pilate. He is incarnate, born of the Virgin Mary, bone of our bones, one of us, flesh for hell's roasting fires. He has suffered, been mocked by soldiers and priests, rejected by family and friends, betrayed by disciples, crucified, executed as the King of the Jews, and is risen from the dead.

Most shocking and unexpected of all His mercy is that He is not angry. He does not hold a grudge. He walks into the upper room and they are reasonably afraid, but He comes speaking peace and breathing out His Spirit.

All this He has done for you. He has been sent by His Father not only for sins, not only for His Father's will, not only to defeat the devil and show who is really good, but He has been sent also for you—to rescue you, to pull you out of the flames of judgment, to redeem you for Himself, to forgive your sins. He could be angry, but He isn't. Nor is He indulgent. He simply is grace incarnate, grace in the flesh, the victor over death, our champion and hero.

Forty-three days after it was finished, He lifted up His pierced hands and blessed them. And while He was blessing them, He rose into the air and was engulfed by a cloud so that they could behold Him no more with their eyes. Among the appearances of our risen Lord in those forty days, this was distinct. As at the other times, He apparently came forth suddenly from the invisible world, but He did not, as on former occasions, suddenly vanish from sight, as if He might shortly return as He had done before. This time He withdrew in a different way; as they watched He rose up into the air. Thus did He indicate that He was no longer with them and therefore those occasional and supernatural appearances, vouchsafed to them since the resurrection, were now at an end.

Yet they were not sad, for we read, "And they worshipped him and returned to Jerusalem with great joy."

They knew that this was not the little while as before the cross, nor the little while since the resurrection. They knew that though their eyes might not see Him, they would now enjoy His blessed presence forever. For His ascension was not simply the physical movement from earth to heaven; rather, His ascension indicated a change of state. His humiliation was over. No longer does He deny Himself, as a man, His divine rights and powers. He is still a man, still one of us, but now, as a man, He fully exercises all His divine attributes. Even as the flames of hell have lost all claim to us, so also can they no longer roast Him. He is no more confined, as a man, by physical space, or subject to hunger or pain. He, as a man, is glorified, and thus opens up heaven for all humanity and especially for those who believe.

That is why the apostles have great joy. They have the Christ in His sacramental presence. In His sacramental presence they have Him closer than they had Him in His humiliation. They have the Scriptures opened to them and the gift and promise of the Father in the Holy Spirit. We have the same. The ascended Christ is with us always, in the baptizing, in the teaching, and in the breaking of the bread. He is present to the end of time, as recorded by St. Matthew, in the apostolic ministry.

Thus do they naturally go to the temple, to church, to continue the work of Moses and Jesus, to preach repentance and the forgiveness of sins in Jesus' name in the shadow of the torn veil. There they point to the mercy seat, no longer hovering over the ark but now in the risen body and blood of Christ, given to His children to eat and to drink. The temple divisions between male and female, Jew and Gentile, have been torn in two. The temple guards have been rendered silent. Jesus lives and is for us in His body and blood.†

In ☩ Jesus' name. Amen.

---

† Much of this exegesis and some lines dependent upon: The Pulpit Commentary: St Luke Vol. II, ed. H. D. M. Spence-Jones (Bellingham, WA: Logos Research Systems, Inc., 2004), p. 277 and vicinity.

The Sixth Sunday after Easter—Exaudi

Ezekiel 36:22-28
1 Peter 4:7-14
St. John 15:26-16:4

In the name of the Father and of the ✠ Son and of the Holy Spirit. Amen.

They will put you out of the synagogues. Indeed, the hour is coming when whoever kills you will think he is offering service to God."

Islamic terrorists kill Christians in the name of their god, as a service to him, as a matter of course. It is a tenet of their religion, clearly and repeatedly taught in their holy books. Those without faith in their Allah or who are disobedient to his laws are to be killed as a service to Allah. To call Islam a religion of peace is to ignore not only its history but also its philosophy, to simply only notice those Muslims who choose not to carry out their religion or follow their books. To be sure, we are glad that there are so many of them who don't really follow Islam, who are disobedient to it in refraining from killing us, but the Muslims who do kill us, who are plotting even now to kill us, do so thinking that it is a service to their god.

I once heard an interview with a member of al-Qaeda. He said of us, of Americans, with disdain, "You love life the way we love death."

He might be right, but to love death is to love evil. It is like loving pain or poverty or hunger.

"They will put you out of the synagogues. Indeed, the hour is coming when whoever kills you will think he is offering service to God," says the Lord. Then He continues, "And they will do these things because they have not known the Father, nor me."

Muslims do not worship the Father of our Lord Jesus Christ by another name. There is no other name under heaven by which men may come to the Father. The Muslims worship their father, the devil.

The reason Muslim terrorists target Christians and think killing them is a service to their god is because they do not know our Lord Jesus Christ or His Father. St. Paul writes that the "things which the Gentiles sacrifice, they sacrifice to devils, and not to God" (1 Cor. 10:20 KJV).

So it should come as no surprise to us that they love death and are unafraid of it. Death will deliver them to their lord, to the one they worshipped while on earth, while hating and killing anyone not like them.

We should always try to listen to the criticism of our enemies, even if we find them despicable. What is it that this member of al-Qaeda found so despicable in us for loving life? It is tempting to think that there is nothing despicable in loving life, but I think he is on to something. We don't really love life, we love living, which is to say that we love ourselves. We love our life. We love it too much, and we love it for the wrong reasons.

Luther rightly points out that whatever we love, trust, or fear can become an idol. We aren't prone to making evil things into idols, like the Muslims loving death, but we are prone to making idols out of good things, like life or health. That is far more subtle and perhaps also more deadly.

Why is it that we spend so much money on medication and doctors? Why is health care the hot topic in our country's politics? Most of the people I talk to assume that if a medical treatment exists—no matter how costly or how unlikely to work—that it is their right to it. They cannot imagine a treatment existing that they would be denied simply because they couldn't afford it.

Health and living can definitely become idols. Repent.

But there is irony here. The instinct to love life, which we might pervert in our fallenness, is a Christian one. It is impossible for us not to cringe at the thought of denying the poor needed health care because they are poor. That, however, is not a problem in Muslim countries. They are fine with the poor being poor. They don't have mercy. It is nearly as bad in Buddhist and Hindu countries. But in those places touched by the Gospel, denying mercy to the poor is a problem.

Why? Because we know sins of omission are sins as surely as sins of commission, and we are called upon to love and serve our neighbors, even those we don't like or who smell bad or who brought it on themselves. We don't ever want to ask, "Lord, when did we see you sick and not visit you?" Because we know it has been often, and our lack is damning.

The terrorist rightly sees our love of living, our fear of death, as weakness. It stands in marked contrast to the obvious truth that many things are worse than death. Our obsession with extending our lives is vain and idolatrous. Even the pagans know that dishonor or vice is worse than death. They are right. Those things are worse than death.

But there is something even worse than dishonor or vice: eternal death, eternal separation from and rebellion against the God of mercy. Kyrie Eleison! Lord, have mercy! We deserve that death. Perhaps, deep in our hearts, that is why we so fear temporal death and love our lives so much.

But here is the Gospel truth: God doesn't send people to hell. They take themselves there. Everyone dies and goes to his lord. The Muslims will be sad, no doubt, to discover how strictly the Koran is kept in hell and what justice truly demands.

We have loved the right things, but for the wrong reasons. We have been seduced by Satan into soft lives and false promises, trying to extend this living death at almost any cost. I always find it outrageous that our doctors don't make house calls, but all of our shut-ins manage to get to the doctor. They can't get to church or family gatherings, but they get to the doctor. Why? Health care and doctors are what matter. The shut-in isn't alone in this. His family does this to him. It is too much of a bother to take him out for anything that isn't really important, and the only thing that is really important is the doctor.

Repent. There is more to life than living.

Do not be afraid of losing life and health. It is not only the Muslims who die and go to their lord. You die and go to your Lord also. No, not everyone who dies goes to a better place. Some, sadly, unnecessarily, die and go to hell—but not you. Your Lord was crucified and raised for your justification. You bear the name of the Holy Trinity upon your forehead and heart. You eat the manna of Jesus' risen body and blood and commune with all the saints and holy angels. You die and go to your Lord, to Jesus Christ and His Father, because He did not love His life but laid it down for yours.

The Lord is risen and ascended. He sends the Holy Spirit to you. He speaks in His Word. You hear His voice, for the Spirit still bears witness of the Son. And this He has done, even warning you of the persecution and temptations that you will face, that you would not fall away. You might die, to be sure, but you won't fall away. He will keep you. He will hold you. He has not died in vain, and He won't give up on you. He won't let life keep you from Him.

And He does not send you to kill anyone, to hate, or to love death. For He Himself is life, and by His grace you love life. By His grace you love and are loved by Him. And if they hate you and even kill you for that, so be it. No, rather, if they hate you and even kill you for that, God be praised, for you go to your Lord.

In ✠ Jesus' name. Amen.

Pentecost

Genesis 11:1-9
Acts 2:1-11
St. John 14:23-31

In the name of the Father and of the ✠ Son and of the Holy Spirit. Amen.

P entecost was one of three major Old Testament feasts. It was celebrated fifty days after Passover and commemorated the giving of the Law at Mt. Sinai.

The miracles of Pentecost mirror that great event. At Pentecost, there was a loud sound throughout the house that all recognized as a sign of the divine presence. At Mt. Sinai, there was thunder. At Pentecost, there were flames that sat upon the disciples but did not burn them. At Mt. Sinai, there was lightning and the glory of God, but Moses was unscathed; the flames that appeared to Moses from the bush hurt neither Moses nor the bush. The disciples felt the Holy Spirit as He filled them and moved them to speak in unlearned languages, even as God had spoken to Moses on the mountain.

But the most distinct thing about Pentecost is the Galilean disciples' proclaiming the mighty works of God in unlearned languages. That miracle is without precedent or parallel in the Old Testament, except in the negative, as we heard this morning: the curse at the tower of Babel. Pentecost is a reversal of Babel, not only in comprehension, but also in reuniting men into one family, namely, the family of God.

But there are other miracles at Pentecost, some not quite so obvious. The disciples had once hidden in fear of the Jews in that same room. The room where the Holy Supper was instituted is now the room where the Holy Spirit comes upon them with a loud sound, flames, and languages. For forty days, the risen Lord had appeared to them in His body, but they had remained mostly confused and afraid, even as He opened the

Scriptures to them. Then He had ascended, departed visibly from them up into the clouds, and they were not afraid or sad. They rejoiced and returned to Jerusalem to wait for the Holy Spirit. They waited, as the Church always waits, in prayer. And then they are not only no longer afraid, but they are bold. When the crowd comes to investigate the great noise, St. Peter walks out and preaches to them without fear, even calling them to account for what they did to the innocent Lord.

When Luther preached against Prince Frederick's relics, he risked his life. But it seems to me that Luther was largely naive. He expected people to be convinced by the Word of God, so he was at least as foolish as he was brave. But when St. Peter walks into the crowd that yelled "crucify" and calls them to account for it, there is no naivety. He knows what they're capable of, and he knows how hard it is for men to believe.

That is the first part of this great miracle. The apostles were changed, emboldened by the Holy Spirit for this purpose: to preach. St. Peter was inspired by the Holy Spirit to preach the death and resurrection of Jesus Christ, and he was bold in his office.

We should note that whether or not Luther was a fool who knew the risk he took, the Lord created faith in Prince Frederick through him. Without Prince Frederick, Luther would have been destroyed. In many ways, of all the important figures of the Reformation, Prince Frederick was the most important. If he hadn't been pious, the whole thing would have stopped before it really began. But this was nothing new. It was the same at Pentecost.

Because that is the second part of the miracle: Some believed. They heard the mighty works of God in their native tongues; they heard God speaking through men. And the same Holy Spirit that had lit upon the apostles, and is always present in the preaching of the Word, came through the preaching and lit upon their hearts, and they believed. We didn't read it this morning (it comes later in Acts 2), but there were thousands that day that were cut to the heart by the Holy Spirit in St. Peter's preaching. They asked, "What shall we do?" St. Peter commanded, "Repent and be baptized every one of you in the name of Jesus Christ for the forgiveness of your sins" (Acts 2:38). Then he promised, "[Y]ou will receive the gift of the Holy Spirit. For the promise is for you and for your children and for all who are far off, everyone whom the Lord our God calls to himself" (Acts 2:38-39). Three thousand were baptized that very day and added to the number of the saints. It was three thousand miracles that day, and the miracle keeps going. Prince Frederick heard St. Peter's preaching in Wittenberg 1500 years later, and you hear it today.

But in the midst of Pentecost miracles, there is still hatred and malice. Some hear the languages and mock the Lord and His disciples in willful, deliberate ignorance, saying, "They are drunk." Not all believed.

The preaching of the Gospel always sounds like drunken speech to the unrepentant. I used to think this was because the good news of God's love sounds ridiculous and impossible to sinners. It seems too good to be true. But yesterday I attended a high school graduation. I don't know when I have ever heard such exaggerated, insane speech. The keynote speaker actually proclaimed that the class of 2012 could cure cancer and solve all the world's problems. There were two hours of such speeches, and most of them could have been delivered to a platoon that had just won the medal of honor or put an end to poverty just by changing the opening address. The things that I heard yesterday were too good to be true. In fact, they weren't true.

But no one seemed bothered by it. I don't think they believed it, but they wanted to and they played along. No one accused any of the speakers of being drunk.

The problem with the Gospel—with the shocking news that God loves and forgives us in Christ Jesus despite our hatred of and rebellion against Him—is not that it is radical and hard to believe; it is that those who preach it believe it. The speaker yesterday was engaged in ritualistic, annual flattery that we've all come to expect. This is what commencement speeches do. But the apostles on Pentecost—and Christians ever since—have been proclaiming the good news of Jesus Christ with actual conviction, and that conviction makes sinners uneasy.

And they should be uneasy. We should be uneasy. We should likewise be like those dwelling in Jerusalem who asked, "What shall we do?" The good news of God's love in Christ is based upon our desperate need for that love. Forgiveness of sins is only good news for sinners. It is only good news if you need it. We are sinners. We need it. And we are bold to say that, in this, we are not alone. We have acted, said, and thought evil and selfish things. We have lied and gossiped. We have cheated and stolen. We have lusted and been proud. We have at least some sense of what is good, of what we should be, but we do not live up to our own standards, let alone to God's holy commandments. We do not have the right to mercy. We do not deserve to be spared punishment, and if we were left on our own, we would be damned. What shall we do?

Repent and be baptized, every one of you. Already baptized? God be praised. Repent and return to your baptism. Circumcise your hearts. Turn from your sin. Throw yourself upon God's mercy. Confess your sins because you are baptized. You have been named with God's own name. You belong to Him. But then, if that is the case, He also belongs to you. He cannot and He will not refuse your call. He has promised to be your God. You have access to Him through prayer, confession and absolution, His Word, and the Holy Communion. Return to His name, to His way, to His promise. Return to Holy Baptism where the Holy Spirit was poured out upon you and where God's own Word was made your inheritance. And there find your Father eager to accept and welcome you home.

This is not the invitation of a drunk man or of someone spouting ritualistic hope for new graduates, but of a sober man full of the Holy Spirit: "[Y]ou will receive the gift of the Holy Spirit. For the promise is for you and for your children and for all who are far off, everyone whom the Lord our God calls to himself" (Acts 2:38-39). And from that same man, quoting another: "[E]veryone who calls on the name of the Lord shall be saved" (Acts 2:21).

Thus was the Law given at Mt. Sinai—that the Lord would be their Lord. Thus was the Spirit given in Jerusalem—that the Lord would be your Lord.

In ✠ Jesus' name. Amen.

The Confession of St. Peter

January 18

Acts 4:8-13
2 Peter 1:1-15
St. Mark 8:27-9:1

In the name of the Father and of the ✣ Son and of the Holy Spirit. Amen.

Our Lord is not vain. He is not like us. He does not Google Himself. So when He asks, "Who do men say that I am?" there is more to it than curiosity.

He wants the Church to be aware of the world's many views of Him. Today many say that our Lord is a prophet. He is honored like Moses in Muslim nations. Many say He was a teacher or a philosopher and then boast of focusing on "the words written in red." This was the strategy of no less than Thomas Jefferson. But Walt Whitman and Mark Twain had much the same idea, and it is still popular.

No one says bad things about Jesus unless he is trying to be offensive or garner attention through shock. People say bad things about the pope, about Martin Luther, about Abraham Lincoln, but never about Jesus. He is universally recognized as a good man who was martyred for His cause. Modern men tell us that they do not hate Jesus; they only hate St. Paul and the Church.

Their opinions of our Lord are not new. To say that our Lord was John, Elijah, or Jeremiah is to say that He was another prophet and no more. There is always room for another prophet. Even the Pharisees were willing to call our Lord "Rabbi." As long as He is a prophet and no more, or even a king or a priest, there is no problem. The problem is if He is the Messiah, God in the flesh, because that changes everything.

St. Peter's answer is not an opinion. It is a confession. That is why our Lord asks. He wants men to confess. "Who do you—that is, all of you—say that I am?" Peter answers for the Church. "You are the One anointed to die our death and ransom us out of hell." That is what it is to be the Christ. "You are the Son of the living God." He is not a believer, though He believed, nor is He an angel, though He brought good news. He is the Son of the living God because He is the only-begotten of the Father. He is God. Thus Peter confesses, "You are the Christ, the Son of the living God. You are God in the flesh, our Messiah, our God, our Man, come to save us."

This confession is not his own. Peter is not so good a theologian as that. No one is. The clever theologians come up with Elijah. That is where cleverness is. In confession, there is no art, no poetry, no clever-ness. The best guesses of men are always off because they somehow always come back to us.

Peter's confession is not revealed by flesh and blood, even his own flesh and blood, but by the Father in heaven. Peter's confession, as confession always is, is a gift.

When we think of Jonah, we think mainly of his burial at sea in the great fish and his resurrection. Yet there is more to Jonah than that. Jonah preached repentance and salvation to the Gentiles. The Church is not built upon miracles as men count miracles, but upon the Son of Jonah. It is built there because the distinction between Jews and Gentiles is gone. The Church is where the Gentiles are baptized and taught. Sins, forgiven on earth, are gone in heaven. The Lord bestows the title "son of God" upon mere men, and Gentiles are washed into Israel. It is an ethnic cleansing of a whole different sort, a cleansing not to wipe Gentiles off the face of the earth as an inferior people, but a cleansing that transforms them into the Lord's people on earth and in heaven. He came only for the lost sheep of Israel, so He makes a people who were no people into His people, into Israel, and there is no Jew or Greek.

In the Spirit, the Father reveals the Son, which is to say this revelation, that Jesus is the Christ, is given in Holy Baptism. Peter didn't dream this up or figure it out by clever exegesis. He is not Joseph Smith. This was revealed to him when Jesus was anointed, which is, of course, what the word Messiah means—"anointed one"—and the Father's voice was heard as the Spirit lit upon our Lord in visible form. When did this revelation become Peter's confession? When Peter was baptized into the same, which is not to say that Peter always knew it. Our confession, by grace, is steadfast. Our knowledge is not. Abraham had trouble remembering who He was and what the promise was. So did Jacob. So did David. So did Elijah. So did Peter, and so do we. Thus when the Lord reveals Himself to us in His Word, we find ourselves thinking, "I've always believed that but never quite knew it before." Knowledge of the faith is always remembering what has already been given and is always ours.

We have but one Lord, one faith, one baptism. Your baptism was none other than Peter's baptism, which was none other than our Lord's baptism, which was nothing less than the Father speaking His approval of you, the Spirit's possession of you, and the marking of you for the cross and resurrection. That there is only one baptism does not mean you shouldn't be baptized multiple times, though you shouldn't, but that there is only one baptism: Jesus' baptism, into which you must be, and are, baptized. Do you not say that Jesus is the Christ, the Son of the Living God? Indeed, and this was not revealed by flesh and blood but by the Father's anointing of the Son with the water and the Spirit at the hand of John, into which you were also baptized—whether you knew it or not.

He is the Christ. You are His beloved.

In ✚ Jesus' name. Amen.

The Presentation of Our Lord

February 2

1 Samuel 1:21-28
Malachi 3:1-4
St. Luke 2:22-40

In the name of the Father and of the ✠ Son and of the Holy Spirit. Amen.

Simeon combined the three characteristics necessary for Old Testament piety. He was *just* in his relation and bearing to God and man. He was *God-fearing*. That word is weakly translated in the ESV as "devout," which is in no way sufficient. Εὐλαβὴς means awe, caution, fear toward God. This caution and fear was held in showing opposition to the boastful self-righteousness and self-confidence of the Pharisees. Above all, however, Simeon held a *longing expectancy* of the end of the age and the fulfillment of the great promises.

He was waiting, explicitly, for the "consolation of Israel." The Holy Spirit, the Consoler, was upon him. Paraclete means consoler. It is the word here used to describe what Simeon was waiting for. He was waiting for the Holy Spiriting of Israel. By that Spirit he had been told that the answer to his heart's longing, the Holy Spiriting of Israel, was present in the world and coming to the temple. Thus, Simeon was there just as the Lord's mother and guardian were bringing the infant Jesus in. He took the Lord into his arms and burst into rapt thanksgiving.

Now, indeed, God had fulfilled His Word. Simeon was not to see death until he had seen the Christ. Seeing the Christ meant that he could die and be at peace.

Some exegetes—who specialize in mechanics and details and have no understanding of the soul of Holy Scripture, who have lost sight of the story and cannot read—might point out to us that the text nowhere says that Simeon himself was old or that he went and died shortly after this account. Those exegetes should be buried naked in ant hills.

The nuance and color of this account is obvious. Simeon had waited a long time. He is the icon of the Old Testament saints. He had been waiting for seven thousand years. After this he has nothing left to wait for—which is to say, nothing to live for. He goes and dies, departs this world in peace right away. No, the Bible doesn't say those things explicitly. But if an exegete can't read the story between the lines, if he can't pay attention to the clues, if he thinks the Holy Scriptures are a blueprint or a geometrical proof, then he is not worth his wages.

Simeon had been waiting for death and waiting to see the Lord's Messiah. That is not two things; it is only one. It is what we all wait for, what the whole Christian Church is eager for, and, also, what the Lord gives a foretaste and foresight of in the Holy Supper.

In Bach's Cantata 82, a cantata on the Nunc Dimitis, we read this paraphrase of Simeon's song: *"Ich habe genug,"* that is, "I have enough."

Even when Germans don't use actual vulgarities, it comes out vulgar. *Ich habe genug.* I have enough. I have seen the Christ. I am ready to go. I am satisfied. Simeon speaks to the Lord of his weariness of this world like a child tired of eating broccoli, pushing the plate away. *Ich habe genug!*

Bach goes on: "I have enough! I have seen Him. My faith and heart have held Him, and now I wish, even today, filled with joy, to divorce this place."

Bach gets it exactly right. Simeon's justice, fear of God, and longing expectancy were all by-products of his faith and love of God. He has had enough of this world, enough of sin, enough of politics and Pharisees and old age. He was ready to go where he belonged, to go home, to be divorced of this place and to be made the newly immaculate and virgin bride of Christ by grace.

The faith that the Lord's Supper encourages and strengthens also creates ever greater dissatisfaction with this world. May we never be satisfied here! May we ever be jealous of those allowed to remain in the temple singing the Lord's praise and of those who have already been translated to heaven! They have come to what we desire.

But this isn't Narnia under the white witch. It is winter. Death is all around us, but we have Christmas. The Lord's Messiah, our salvation, has come into the world, announced by angels, greeted by shepherds and Gentile sages. Now Epiphany is over. The Presentation marks the end. We are ready for Lent. But Christ is still present. Once Christmas comes, it never leaves.

Let us set our faces toward Jerusalem in solemnity and confidence, knowing the end not just of His story, and the purpose of His suffering and death, but also of our own, that like Simeon before us, for we too shall depart in peace, divorced from this place, and become the virgin bride of Christ by grace.

In ✠ Jesus' name. Amen.

Saint Matthias, Apostle

February 24

Isaiah 66:1-2
Acts 1:15-26
St. Matthew 11:25-30

In the name of the Father and of the ✚ Son and of the Holy Spirit. Amen.

The betrayer was replaced by the forgotten.

St. Matthias was put into the office that Judas had forfeited through impenitence and suicide. But who remembers Matthias? We remember Judas. We forget Matthias.

Judas is a criminal of the worst sort. He betrays his friend. He causes the abuse and then the unjust execution of an innocent man who had only been good to him.

Matthias, however, seems to do nothing noteworthy. The Bible records his installation as a bishop of the Church but then never mentions him again. Even the legends are sketchy. We know more about St. Lucy—who may not even have been an actual person—than we do about Matthias.

Most likely, St. Matthias simply went about the work of the ministry in a quiet way, baptizing, teaching, and administering the Sacrament as he was called to do. And that, it seems, is not noteworthy.

Something is wrong with us. I suspect it is the same thing that loves gossip and VH1 "Behind the Music" specials. We are thrilled to watch other people fail. So we remember Judas and forget Matthias.

It is at once shocking and comforting to hear that Judas' ministry was not dissolved by his wicked death. It almost seems as though it should have been, as though that vile act disproved God's love and faithfulness. But death cannot defeat life: Jesus lives. The office of apostle and bishop did not depend on Judas or his actions. It did not even depend upon his faith. This devil of a man, Judas, held the office because he was put into it by the grace of Jesus Christ who has authority on heaven and earth, and not because he was good.

So also Matthias served in the same way: not according to his own merit, but by God's grace. And when Matthias was elected by God, through the drawing of lots, he was placed into an already existing office. In some ways every pastor since Matthias is serving in the office of Judas. We all follow Matthias, for none of us was numbered in the original twelve.

This is as it should be. For only God is good, and it is His office. Only He confers the holy office and through it, His glorious riches. The preachers merely distribute such good things. The goodness of what they distribute does not come from them or their goodness, but from the goodness of God.

In this we should take great comfort: The validity of the preaching and the Sacraments does not depend on the holiness of the bishops, but on the holiness of God. In this, Matthias should be forgotten, but the office that God has given and the good He bestows through it should be remembered.†

In ✠ Jesus' name. Amen.

---

† The ideas in this sermon were borrowed, in part, from a devotion by Rev. Dr. Scott Murray and his Memorial Moments 2006.

The Feast of the Annunciation

March 25

Isaiah 7:10-14
St. Luke 1:26-38

In the name of the Father and of the ✠ Son and of the Holy Spirit. Amen.

H e shall reign over the house of Jacob for ever; and of his kingdom there shall be no end" (KJV).

The Holy Spirit overshadowed the peasant virgin of King David's line. The Word of God entered into her ear and impregnated her with the second person of the Holy Trinity. Eve had a Seed. And by that holy Seed in her womb, St. Mary found favor with God and was freed from her fear. In this way, God took up human flesh in order to redeem human flesh by sacrifice of that flesh in perfect love. His name can only be "Yahweh saves," that is, Joshua, Jesus.

"He shall reign over the house of Jacob for ever; and of his kingdom there shall be no end."

St. Mary, most blessed of all women, is of the house of Jacob. She is an Israelite of Israelites, of the tribe of Judah. Her Son rules her with servile compliance. He makes water into wine to please her before His time. When He dies, He hands her care over to the disciple whom He loves, that she should be sustained in her penury and sorrow.

He rules forever in the house of Jacob by washing the feet of His disciples, turning the other cheek, and submitting to Pilate's true words but false judgment, "King of the Jews." He makes new Israelites, adopts heathen people into Jacob's house that they too would learn to wrestle with Him, limping away but with a blessing. He calls the sanctified

Canaanite prostitute Rahab "mother" and "daughter." He calls the Syrophoenician woman "sister," and the Roman Centurion, He calls "Sir."

"He shall reign over the house of Jacob for ever; and of his kingdom there shall be no end."

Let it also be unto us according to this Word, that the Church in her old age might still conceive and bear sons of grace, a people who were no people, who are defined not by continent of origin, country of habitation, or color of skin but by the promise made to Abraham; that we might enter into the kingdom of glory by way of the cross and be ruled forever in mercy; that we too should be free from fear and ever eager for the completion of what He has begun in us in Holy Baptism.

Let us be handmaidens of the Lord, doorkeepers for the house of God, lap-dogs eating crumbs from the master's table. Let us be those who find favor and reconciliation in the everlasting goodness that has sent "God with us" in the Son of Mary, "God for us" on Rome's wicked cross, and "God in us" through the body hidden in bread that descended into hell, was raised from the dead, and now rules at the right hand of His Father.

"He shall reign over the house of Jacob for ever; and of his kingdom there shall be no end."

Let us ever be overshadowed by that Holy Spirit, impregnated by that Holy Word, and begotten anew by that Holy Father, that we might ever bear the title of all grace and best inheritance: Christian.

In ✠ Jesus' name. Amen.

Saint Mark, Evangelist

April 25

Ezekiel 1:10-14
St. Mark 1:1-15

In the name of the Father and of the ✠ Son and of the Holy Spirit. Amen.

In the Church, we make distinctions with honorary titles that have lost their distinctions in modern English. In the Church, an evangelist is someone who wrote one of the four Gospels. There are only four evangelists. Billy Graham is not one of them. St. Mark is.

The reason for this academic-sounding distinction—not wanting everyone to lay claim to a title reserved for four specific individuals—is the uniqueness of the Word of God and the reverence we owe it. We honor those human authors chosen by God for this great task. Not every Christian has been a pastor, a patriarch, a prophet, an apostle, or an evangelist. And while all Christians, even Christians who lived and believed before the time of Christ's birth, share the common office of priest, their other offices are distinct. Even those pressed by God into His Service as stewards of His Word have distinctions according to time and call.

I am honored and humbled that God has called me to preach and administer for Him, in His stead, to His people, the gifts of the New Testament, but I am not a prophet. I did not receive a direct call from God, nor do I enjoy direct revelation from God. And I am not given to record further revelation from Him. I am dependent upon His Word which has come through the prophets and apostles. In the same way, I don't rule as the patriarchs and judges did. The ministry of the Old Testament was in ways greater than the ministry in which I serve. But they never preached on the incarnation, death, and resurrection of Jesus Christ born of Mary the way I can because I know details that they didn't. Nor did they ever name someone with God's own name in Holy Baptism, washing clean sinners in the healing fountain that flows from the side of Christ. They never consecrated bread and wine into His body and blood. They and I share the same office, but it is distinct by time and call and by the specific duties and privileges accorded to it.

Neither do we modern pastors have the gift of the Holy Spirit in the same way that the apostles did. We don't administer supernatural healing, speak in unlearned languages, or perform other miracles. And, finally, we write no Gospel. We are utterly dependent upon the records of the apostles in the New Testament and the records of the prophets in the Old Testament.

But dependency is not a bad thing. Indeed, we are weak, but when we are weak—when we have only the Word of God and nothing else, when we can't "think for ourselves" and imagine our own god after our own design, but must submit to the incomprehensible revealed will of the Almighty—then we are strong. For God's inspired and inerrant Word is the source and norm of all our doctrine and life. It is the power of God for salvation. It changes the hearts of men. It turns them, brings them out of death to life. It forgives, restores, and comforts. For it reveals God's desire for man, that man again be declared good, again belong to Him, and all this by undeserved kindness and love found in the death and resurrection of Jesus Christ, God incarnate to die. And of all these revelations, of all this divine Word and truth, the greatest are the biographies of our Salvation, the Holy Gospels.

Thus, we honor the evangelists who have served God by serving us, by delivering unto us the preaching of Jesus, the events of His life and ministry, His miracles and travels, His sorrows and joys, His cruel, atoning death where death was destroyed and life was raised again to life that we might live. They have given us the Gospel, the good news of God's love in Jesus.

All of Holy Scripture has the power and authority to make us wise for salvation through faith in Christ Jesus. "All Scripture is breathed out by God and profitable for teaching, for reproof, for correction, and for training in righteousness, that the man of God may be complete, equipped for every good work" (2 Tim. 3:16-17). But the Gospels give us the very events and words of our Lord's incarnation, and thus we afford them more honor in the Divine Service, standing when they are read, and thus, too, do we afford their writers more honor and a special title.

Thanks and praise be to God for all the writers of Holy Scripture who have served us so ably by His grace. Thanks and praise be to God for all ministers of His Word who have delivered unto us the joy of heaven with absolving words from on high. Thanks and praise be to God, especially this day, for St. Mark and the blessed legacy that God has left for us through his hand.

In ✠ Jesus' name. Amen.

Scripture Index

New Testament

CPSIA information can be obtained at www.ICGtesting.com
Printed in the USA
BVOW03s1744230714

360191BV00011B/507/P

9 781934 328071